What People ~~are saying~~
about *Threshold Bible Study*

"Falling in love with the sacred Scriptures enables us to fall in deeper love with our loving God. *Threshold Bible Study* helps us see the Word of God alive in us and among us."
🔲 **ARCHBISHOP GREGORY M. AYMOND**, *Archbishop of New Orleans*

"The books in Stephen Binz's *Threshold Bible Study* read like *lectio divina* meditations from the monastic tradition, but with fascinating historical insights about the biblical characters and authors. He has a gift for making these ancient texts speak an urgent but compelling word to us today, inviting us to read ourselves into the great drama of salvation history. He nourishes the roots of our Christian faith in the rich soil of Judaism, and he presents the Bible as a single fountain with an endlessly fresh supply of water for anyone thirsting for the Lord."
🔲 **THOMAS ESPOSITO, O. CIST.**, *Professor of Theology, University of Dallas*

"*Threshold Bible Study* enables Catholics to read, with greater understanding, the Bible in the Church."
🔲 **FRANCIS CARDINAL GEORGE, OMI**, *the late Archbishop Emeritus of Chicago*

"The Church has called Scripture a 'font' and 'wellspring' for the spiritual life. *Threshold Bible Study* is one of the best sources for tapping into the biblical font. *Threshold Bible Study* offers you an encounter with the word that will make your heart come alive."
🔲 **TIM GRAY**, *President of the Augustine Institute, Denver*

"*Threshold Bible Study* offers solid scholarship and spiritual depth. It can be counted on for lively individual study and prayer, even while it offers spiritual riches to deepen communal conversation and reflection among the people of God."
🔲 **SCOTT HAHN**, *Founder and President, St. Paul Center for Biblical Theology*

"Stephen Binz's *Threshold Bible Study* expertly blends deep scholarly insight with warm, approachable language, perfectly suiting both group and individual study. Binz's engaging style makes profound spiritual truths accessible and relatable, offering a transformative experience for those seeking to deepen their faith through an encounter with sacred Scripture. This series is a treasure for anyone looking to explore the Bible in a fresh and life-changing way. It serves as a beautiful gateway of grace for those yearning to enrich their faith journey."
🔲 **KRIS MCGREGOR**, *founder and director of DiscerningHearts.com and host of "Inside the Pages"*

"*Threshold Bible Study* is an enriching and enlightening approach to understanding the rich faith which the Scriptures hold for us today. Written in a clear and concise style, *Threshold Bible Study* presents solid contemporary biblical scholarship, offers questions for reflection and/or discussion, and then demonstrates a way to pray from the Scriptures. All these elements work together to offer the reader a wonderful insight into how the sacred texts of our faith can touch our lives in a profound and practical way today. I heartily recommend this series to both individuals and Bible study groups."

ABBOT GREGORY J. POLAN, OSB, *Conception Abbey,*
Abbot Primate of the Benedictine Order

"*Threshold Bible Study* guides readers to 'do justice, love kindness, and walk humbly with God,' reflecting on Scripture and acting on its prophetic call. Stephen Binz uses his biblical scholarship and passion for God's word to show others how to take on the mind and heart of Jesus through a meditative reading of Scripture. I recommend this approach to Bible study because it spotlights key themes of biblical revelation and underscores their contemporary importance."

HELEN PREJEAN, CSJ, *Activist in opposition to the death penalty,*
author of **Dead Man Walking** *and* **River of Fire**, *New Orleans*

"Stephen J. Binz is a consistently outstanding Catholic educator and communicator whose books on the study and application of Scripture have thoroughly enriched my Christian understanding. In our fast-moving, often confusing times, his ability to help us examine and comprehend the truth through all the noise is especially needed and valuable."

ELIZABETH SCALIA, *writer and blogger as The Anchoress*

"Stephen Binz has created an essential resource for the new evangelization rooted in the discipleship process that helps participants to unpack the treasures of the Scriptures in an engaging and accessible manner. *Threshold Bible Study* connects faith learning to faithful living, leading one to a deeper relationship with Christ and his body, the Church."

JULIANNE STANZ, *Director of New Evangelization, Diocese of Green Bay*

"*Threshold Bible Study* draws readers into an experience of the word of God through intricately researched historical details along with a profound spirituality of the Scriptures. Encountering Christ through the Word provides light for our lives, hope for our hearts, and passion to share this word with everyone. Thanks to Stephen Binz's scholarship, readers can delve deeply into God's love letter to humanity!"

SR. NANCY USSELMANN, FSP, *Director of Pauline Center for Media Studies*

Mary

Royal
Mother of
the Messiah

Stephen J. Binz

TWENTY-THIRD PUBLICATIONS
twentythirdpublications.com

TWENTY-THIRD PUBLICATIONS
977 Hartford Turnpike Unit A
Waterford, CT 06385
(860) 437-3012 or (800) 321-0411
www.twentythirdpublications.com

ISBN: 978-1-62785-810-6
Printed in the U.S.A.

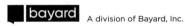 A division of Bayard, Inc.

Contents

LESSONS 13–18

LESSONS 19–24

LESSONS 25–30

How to Use
Threshold Bible Study

T hreshold Bible Study is a dynamic, informative, inspiring, and
life-changing series that helps you learn about Scripture in a whole
new way. Each book will help you explore new dimensions of faith
and discover deeper insights for your life as a disciple of Jesus.

The threshold is a place of transition. The threshold of God's word invites you
to enter that place where God's truth, goodness, and beauty can shine into your
life and fill your mind and heart. Through the Holy Spirit, the threshold becomes
holy ground, sacred space, and graced time. God can teach you best at the threshold, because God opens your life to his word and fills you with the Spirit of truth.

With *Threshold Bible Study*, each topic or book of the Bible is approached in a
thematic way. You will understand and reflect on the biblical texts through over-
arching themes derived from biblical theology. Through this method, the study
of Scripture will impact your life in a unique way and transform you from within.

These books are designed for maximum flexibility. Each study is presented in a workbook format, with sections for reading, reflecting, writing,
discussing, and praying. Each *Threshold* book contains thirty lessons, which
you can use for your daily study over the course of a month or which can be
divided into six lessons per week, providing a group study of six weekly ses-
sions. These studies are ideal for Bible study groups, small Christian commu-
nities, adult faith formation, student groups, Sunday school, neighborhood
groups, and family reading, as well as for individual learning.

The commentary that follows each biblical passage launches your reflection on that passage and helps you begin to see its significance within the
context of your contemporary experience. The questions following the commentary challenge you to understand the passage more fully and apply it to
your own life. Space for writing after each question is ideal for personal study
and also allows group participants to prepare for the weekly discussion. The
prayer helps conclude your study each day by integrating your learning into
your relationship with God.

The method of *Threshold Bible Study* is rooted in the ancient tradition of
lectio divina, whereby studying the Bible becomes a means of deeper intimacy
with God and a transformed life. Reading and interpreting the text (*lectio*) is

followed by reflective meditation on its message (*meditatio*). This reading and reflecting flows into prayer from the heart (*oratio* and *contemplatio*). In this way, one listens to God through the Scripture and then responds to God in prayer.

This ancient method assures you that Bible study is a matter of both the mind and the heart. It is not just an intellectual exercise to learn more and be able to discuss the Bible with others. It is, more importantly, a transforming experience. Reflecting on God's word, guided by the Holy Spirit, illumines the mind with wisdom and stirs the heart with zeal.

Following the personal Bible study, *Threshold Bible Study* offers ways to extend personal *lectio divina* into a weekly conversation with others. This communal experience will allow participants to enhance their appreciation of the message and build up a spiritual community (*collatio*). The end result will be to increase not only individual faith but also faithful witness in the context of daily life (*operatio*).

When bringing *Threshold Bible Study* to a church community, try to make every effort to include as many people as possible. Many will want to study on their own; others will want to study with family, a group of friends, or a few work associates; some may want to commit themselves to share insights through a weekly conference call, daily text messaging, or an online social network; and others will want to gather weekly in established small groups.

By encouraging *Threshold Bible Study* and respecting the many ways people desire to make Bible study a regular part of their lives, you will widen the number of people in your church community who study the Bible regularly in whatever way they are able in their busy lives. Simply sign up people at the Sunday services and order bulk quantities for your church. Encourage people to follow the daily study as faithfully as they can. This encouragement can be through Sunday announcements, notices in parish publications, support on the church website, and other creative invitations and motivations.

Through the spiritual disciplines of Scripture reading, study, reflection, conversation, and prayer, *Threshold Bible Study* will help you experience God's grace more abundantly and root your life more deeply in Christ. The risen Jesus said: "Listen! I am standing at the door, knocking; if you hear my voice and open the door, I will come in to you and eat with you, and you with me" (Rev 3:20). Listen to the word of God, open the door, and cross the threshold to an unimaginable dwelling with God!

SUGGESTIONS FOR INDIVIDUAL STUDY

- Make your Bible reading a time of prayer. Ask for God's guidance as you read the Scriptures.

- Try to study daily, or as often as possible according to the circumstances of your life.

- Read the Bible passage carefully, trying to understand both its meaning and its personal application as you read. Some persons find it helpful to read the passage aloud.

- Read the passage in another Bible translation. Each version adds to your understanding of the original text.

- Allow the commentary to help you comprehend and apply the scriptural text. The commentary is only a beginning, not the last word, on the meaning of the passage.

- After reflecting on each question, write out your responses. The very act of writing will help you clarify your thoughts, bring new insights, and amplify your understanding.

- As you reflect on your answers, think about how you can live God's word in the context of your daily life.

- Conclude each daily lesson by reading the prayer and continuing with your own prayer from the heart.

- Make sure your reflections and prayers are matters of both the mind and the heart. A true encounter with God's word is always a transforming experience.

- Choose a word or a phrase from the lesson to carry with you throughout the day as a reminder of your encounter with God's life-changing word.

- For additional insights and affirmation, share your learning experience with at least one other person whom you trust. The ideal way to share learning is in a small group that meets regularly.

SUGGESTIONS FOR GROUP STUDY

- Meet regularly; weekly is ideal. Try to be on time and make attendance a high priority for the sake of the group. The average group meets for about an hour.

- Open each session with a prepared prayer, a song, or a reflection. Find some appropriate way to bring the group from the workaday world into a sacred time of graced sharing.

- If you have not been together before, name tags are very helpful as a group begins to become acquainted with the other group members.

- Spend the first session getting acquainted with one another, reading the Introduction aloud, and discussing the questions that follow.

- Appoint a group facilitator to provide guidance to the discussion. The role of facilitator may rotate among members each week. The facilitator simply keeps the discussion on track; each person shares responsibility for the group. There is no need for the facilitator to be a trained teacher.

- Try to study the six lessons on your own during the week. When you have done your own reflection and written your own answers, you will be better prepared to discuss the six scriptural lessons with the group. If you have not had an opportunity to study the passages during the week, meet with the group anyway to share support and insights.

- Participate in the discussion as much as you are able, offering your thoughts, insights, feelings, and decisions. You learn by sharing with others the fruits of your study.

- Be careful not to dominate the discussion. It is important that everyone in the group be offered an equal opportunity to share the results of their work. Try to link what you say to the comments of others so that the group remains on the topic.

- When discussing your own personal thoughts or feelings, use "I" language. Be as personal and honest as appropriate and be very cautious about giving advice to others.

- Listen attentively to the other members of the group so as to learn from their insights. The words of the Bible affect each person in a different way, so a group provides a wealth of understanding for each member.

- Don't fear silence. Silence in a group is as important as silence in personal study. It allows individuals time to listen to the voice of God's Spirit and the opportunity to form their thoughts before they speak.

- Solicit several responses for each question. The thoughts of different people will build on the answers of others and will lead to deeper insights for all.

- Don't fear controversy. Differences of opinions are a sign of a healthy and honest group. If you cannot resolve an issue, continue on, agreeing to disagree. There is probably some truth in each viewpoint.

- Discuss the questions that seem most important for the group. There is no need to cover all the questions in the group session.

- Realize that some questions about the Bible cannot be resolved, even by experts. Don't get stuck on some issue for which there are no clear answers.

- Whatever is said in the group is said in confidence and should be regarded as such.

- Pray as a group in whatever way feels comfortable. Pray for the members of your group throughout the week.

Schedule for Group Study

Session 1: Introduction   Date: _____

Session 2: Lessons 1–6   Date: _____

Session 3: Lessons 7–12   Date: _____

Session 4: Lessons 13–18   Date: _____

Session 5: Lessons 19–24   Date: _____

Session 6: Lessons 25–30   Date: _____

"Surely, from now on all generations will call me blessed; for the Mighty One has done great things for me, and holy is his name." LUKE 1:48–49

Mary: Royal Mother of the Messiah

Mary will never impede our drawing close to God. On the contrary, the more we get to know and love the Blessed Virgin Mary, the more we come to know and love the Father, the Son, and the Holy Spirit. There is a unique relationship between the Triune God and this holy woman, a relationship that lasts forever. Mary's perfect relationship with the persons of the Trinity, as described through the gospel accounts, enriches our own desire for union with God and for a more intimate sharing in the divine nature. She is the beloved daughter of the eternal Father, the tender mother of the incarnate Son, and the devoted spouse of the Holy Spirit. If we wish to follow Mary into communion with the Trinity, then we must get to know her and imitate her example.

As daughter of the Father, Mary is a member of God's people Israel. United with God in covenant, she is devoted to the Torah and attentive to the prophets. The psalms of her people fill her mind and heart. Because she is a woman focused on God's word, she is ready and receptive when God's plan is revealed to her through the angel. She responds with complete assent: "Here am I, the servant of the Lord; let it be with me according to your word" (Luke 1:38). Because God is our Creator, when we submit to the Father's will, we consent to what we were made to be. Mary's submission to God was so complete that it mirrors Christ's own self-denial in his Passion: "Not my will but yours be done" (Luke 22:42). Mary gave herself totally and she conceived the Son of God through the power of the Holy Spirit.

Mary's maternal cooperation with Jesus in his mission of redemption begins at the moment of his conception. From all eternity God chose for the mother of his Son a daughter of Israel, a young Jewish woman of Nazareth in Galilee,

1

a virgin betrothed to a man whose name was Joseph of the house of David. As mother of the Messiah, she brings him to the world, receiving the ancient title *Theotokos*, the God-Bearer, the one who gives birth to God on earth. Mary is far more than a biological instrument for his birth. God is incarnate from her flesh, "born of the Virgin Mary," made from her own bodily humanity, in solidarity with all the people of the world. Her maternal sharing in the ministry of her Son continues throughout his adult life, from Cana to the cross, and into the life of the church. The mother of Christ becomes the mother of his disciples, the mother of mercy, and the mother of the church.

What seemed unthinkable—a real union between God who is pure spirit and humanity—took place through the working of the Holy Spirit. As the angel told Mary, with God nothing is impossible. As the cloud of God's presence came down and the glory of the Lord filled the ancient tabernacle, so the Holy Spirit came upon Mary and the power of the Most High overshadowed her.

Mary shows us the way to participate more richly in the divine nature (2 Pet 1:4). By submitting ourselves to the will of the Father, sharing in the redeeming mission of the Son, and uniting ourselves to the movements of the Holy Spirit, we gradually grow in holiness and enter the new creation. The glorified Mary experiences eternal life much like we will at the end of that process. We, too, will live with Christ and reign with him (2 Tim 2:11–12). We will receive, like her, the imperishable crown of glory. We will love each other powerfully and fruit-fully, as she does. We, too, will be sinless. We shall be like him, for we shall see him as he is (1 John 3:2). We will be redeemed, sanctified, and glorified.

In her hearing and pondering the Scriptures, Mary has become a model for us. As we study and contemplate Mary through the power of the living word, we will encounter her not as a character in a book but as a mother, mentor, and inspiration. Let us allow her to love us, guide us, teach us, and bring us close to her Son. For all her dignity, all her greatness, comes from him, and from him alone. The surest path to knowing and loving Jesus is through his mother Mary.

Reflection and discussion

- How does Mary lead me to share more intimately in the life of God?

- What do I want to understand better about Mary?

Regal Images of the Blessed Virgin Mary

The Christian tradition has gathered witnesses to the royal dignity of Mary in apostolic documents, prayers of the liturgy, theological writings, works of art and music, and popular devotion. Poets, painters, sculptors, composers, architects, and saints have given honor to Mary under her many noble titles through countless verbal and artistic images.

The noble majesty of Mary is founded upon her divine motherhood. The archangel Gabriel was the first to proclaim Mary as the royal mother of Israel's king. Her son would be "the Son of the Most High," and God would give him "the throne of his ancestor David." He would reign forever and "of his kingdom there will be no end" (Luke 1:32–33). Mary herself is revealed by Elizabeth to be "mother of my Lord," the mother of the one who would be King and Lord of all.

In ancient Israel, the queen was not the wife of the king (for indeed the king often had many wives) but rather the king's mother. This royal mother not only gave birth to her noble son but also served as a real participant in the reign of her son. The king crowned the queen mother and provided a throne for her at his right hand. She served as a counselor to the king and as an advocate for the people, hearing their petitions and presenting them to the king. Since Jesus is the anointed king of the line of David, the royal Messiah of his people, the New Testament depicts Mary as the queen mother and advocate in the kingdom of Christ.

As Mother of the Lord, Mary is always subordinate to her divine Son, yet she truly participates in Christ's reign. With the kingdom of God at hand, Mary in the gospels shares intimately in her Son's victorious work of redemption. Accepting God's word, she offers her entire bodily self to give birth to the Savior. She perseveres through great human suffering as his mother. She initiates his public ministry at the wedding feast of Cana, interceding for the bridal couple and placing their needs in the hands of her Son. Received as mother of all disciples beneath the cross of Jesus and continuing her maternal advocacy into the beginnings of the church at Pentecost, Mary is shown to be the royal mother of the Messiah and mother of his church.

The royal realm in which Mary reigns is unlike worldly kingdoms based on political, economic, or military power. Christ is exalted by the Father and enthroned over all things through becoming a slave, being obedient unto death on a cross. Mary's queenship and advocacy is a participation in Christ's kingship and is rooted in humility, service, and sacrifice. It is precisely in her lowliness as the Lord's servant that God has exalted her. She is uniquely joined to her Son's triumph through her divine maternity and her unique cooperation in his redemptive work. With the heart of a mother, Mary extends her care to all her children: protecting, guiding, and powerfully interceding for them before the throne of her Son. Her singular desire and petition is the salvation of all the family of God.

Mary's queenship is not something far removed from the Christian life, an exalted position in heaven that we may only honor from a distance. The Scriptures attest that Christ promised all his faithful disciples a share in his reign, assuring all who continue with him through trials and die with him will have a place in his kingdom. As a true disciple of Jesus, Mary shares in the kingdom of her Son in communion with all Christians. In the context of the whole people of God, Mary's queenship becomes not only a source of maternal assistance but a model for all to follow. We can look to her as the archetype of that glorified state that all faithful disciples will enter. By imitating her humble service, hearing the word of God and doing it, and persevering throughout life in the following of her Son, we hope to have a share in that same kingdom of God.

As we read and ponder these Scriptures, we may contemplate Mary, seated beside the King of ages, shining forth as mother of Christ, advocate of her children, and queen of heaven and earth. She who taught her Son to pray and aided the beginnings of the church by her prayer now implores her Son in the fellowship of all the saints and angels. We may join with Mary today and every day, pleading to the Father, "Thy kingdom come."

Reflection and discussion
- Why do Christians look upon Mary as a royal mother?

- What are some of my favorite depictions of Mary in painting, sculpture, film, and other media?

Miriam of Nazareth and Jerusalem

As we ponder the many regal titles of Mary, we must not allow them to obscure her simple humanity and her closeness to us. The gospels offer us the image of a strong, resilient, and self-possessed woman. Mary's journey of faith was a struggle. The first time Mary opens her mouth in the New Testament, it is to question God's messenger. "How can this be, since I am a virgin?" she asks, after the angel reveals God's plan for the Messiah's mother. Like all of us who ponder in the face of a life-altering change, she is confused. The angel's news upends whatever ordinary life she has imagined for herself and puts her on a totally different and unpredictable course.

After the angel explains, Mary makes her decision. She says yes. "Let it be done with me according to your word." The peasant maiden decides courageously on her own, without recourse to the male authorities of her day. She takes counsel with her own soul, and in a moment of outrageous self-determining autonomy, she decides to embrace it. She's ready to hand over her future, take up an unimaginable calling, and cope with its lifetime of challenges. She trusted the divine messenger who assured her that "nothing will be impossible with God."

Although we often see Mary depicted as a fair-skinned beauty queen with the most delicate features, she was most certainly a young woman of her time and place. With olive skin, brown eyes, and raven hair, she looked more like Middle Eastern women today. Given the everyday routines of peasant life, she would have had a muscular body shaped by hard daily labor. Although blessed by heaven, she was a daughter of earth. Everything authentically human was present in her.

In the households and villages of Galilee, families occupied a house of two or three small rooms, often extending from a small cave in the hillside. These dwellings were made of native stone, held together by a mortar of mud and pebbles. Doors were framed in wood and covered with mats or curtains. Floors consisted of packed earth, and roofs were constructed of bundles of reeds tied over beams of wood.

Three or four of these dwellings, inhabited by extended family and close kinship groups, were built around a courtyard. In this space open to the sky, the families shared a millstone for grinding grain, a cistern for holding water, and an open-air oven for cooking. Villages normally used a common threshing floor, olive press, and wine press. The everyday diet consisted of grain and olive oil, supplemented with fruits, vegetables, and wine, with milk products for families with a flock of sheep and goats. Village life involved a network of relationships and shared skills for processing the harvest, repairing homes, midwifing, caring for children, tending the sick, and a host of other contingencies. Illnesses were common; infant mortality and a short life expectancy were facts of life.

Mary's daily life was typical of the women of Nazareth. Providing food was a major factor in her daily schedule. Most families had a plot of land for growing wheat, barley, olives, and grapes, with a garden for beans and vegetables, along with trees for figs, dates, and nuts. Harvested crops needed to be processed into forms that would not spoil and could be used out of season. Women spent lots of time threshing, grinding, pitting, and pounding foodstuffs to insure a year-round supply. Another area of women's labor was the provision of clothing for the family. After the men sheared the sheep, the women engaged in the tasks of carding wool, spinning thread, weaving cloth, and sewing garments. Women also made pottery and baskets for household needs. All these tasks absorbed most of the waking hours of the day.

As a Jewish woman, Mary lived a hardscrabble life in the land of her ancestors now occupied by a foreign empire. A descendant of Abraham and Sarah, her faith was formed by the covenant formed at Mount Sinai and nourished by the Scriptures, prayers, feasts, and Torah precepts of the Jewish tradition. She looked toward Jerusalem and its temple as she prayed and anticipated the next pilgrimage, but she feared the inevitable collision of her people with Roman imperial might. She was sustained by messianic hope for the future while the coming of God's kingdom filled her heart.

Jewish women like Mary transmitted to their children the culture, beliefs, and values of their religious heritage. Daily life was marked by the practice of evening and morning prayer, "when you lie down and when you rise up." The rhythm of the week was blessed by sabbath observance from sundown Friday to sundown Saturday, a time of rest, sabbath rituals, reflection on Scripture, and leisure. The years were marked by the annual feasts of Passover (Pesach), Pentecost (Shavuot), and Tabernacles (Sukkot). These festivals were normally celebrated in homes and villages, but on occasion families would travel to Jerusalem on pilgrimage, chanting the psalms and ascending to the gates of the city to participate in days of sacrificial offerings and sacred feasting.

Life did not treat Mary gently. To say that she was full of grace and free from sin does not mean that she never worried or that she did not suffer. She had to find her way from stage to stage of her life's journey, through tears and distress, courage and joy, agony and grief. Young, inexperienced, pregnant, and poor, she was forced to leave home. Without money, comfort, or adequate care, she gave birth in an unkept place. She becomes an image of hope for those who feel they have been cheated of their lives. Her neighbors, by and large, didn't accept her Son. The large crowds of his early ministry dwindled as Jesus disappointed their expectations. But Mary was still there with him at the cross, and she was right there in the upper room praying with the others to become the witnesses Jesus told them to be.

Reflection and discussion

- How does reflecting on the struggles of Mary's everyday life help me to feel close to her?

- Which of Mary's virtues do I most want to imitate?

Learning from Mary

The Madonna venerated on our altars is the poor and humble maiden of Nazareth. Far different from the saccharine and timid temperament with which she is too often depicted, Mary made courageous choices and worked to encourage and strengthen the faith of others. She did not hesitate to proclaim that God vindicates the oppressed and vulnerable, removing the powerful of the world from their privileged positions. In addition to being the biological mother of Jesus and the spiritual mother of his disciples, Mary is also the ideal disciple of Jesus and model for his church. She is a mentor of faith, urging us along, an example for us to imitate.

Because Mary is both virgin and mother, both obedient daughter of God and liberating example for God's people, and both peasant of Nazareth and queen mother of God's kingdom, she opens revolutionary options for God's people. Women and men are able to envision a transformed world, free from oppression and coercion.

The virginity of Mary expresses more than the absence of sexual relations. Through Mary, virginity conveys autonomy, purity of heart, and resistance against forces of domination. In a culture that conscripted young women into marriage and childbearing as their duty, virginity offers women an empowering and liberating alternative. Mary's virginity offers Christian women the option of choosing a more independent lifestyle that includes private time, cultivation of the mind, and spiritual life in community.

Likewise, the motherhood of Mary expresses more than giving biological birth to Jesus. Her royal motherhood stresses that Mary nurtures the life of all God's children, cares for all with her fierce protective instincts, and enhances the dignity of all women who give life to others. As a loving mother, Mary is eager to help her children become everything God created them to be. Mary's motherhood offers Christian women a beautiful understanding of childbearing, but it also helps them understand that their worth is not dependent on having children and that their identity is not exhausted in their childrearing.

Mary is the most celebrated woman in the Christian tradition, radiating the many facets of whole and mature womanhood. She is the flowering of God's new creation manifested in the church. In her the virgin birth of the Son of God can be celebrated as expressing a new order where tired conventions can be rethought and renewed and where oppressive structures are overcome. As Mary continues to live her vocation as Mother of the Lord, she also fulfills her vocation as Mother of the Church.

Because of Mary's preservation from sin throughout her life (The Immaculate Conception) and the glorious conclusion of her earthly life (The Assumption), Mary is far ahead of the rest of us spiritually. Yet, she uses her position for our benefit, interceding to the Lord for us, and even appearing from time to time to strengthen the church on earth. As model of the church, she signifies for all God's people their own call to be fully committed in faithful and loving union with Christ. She personifies the whole church redeemed by God's grace, standing as a sure sign of solace and hope for God's pilgrim people.

When we go to Mary, accept her help, and desire to imitate her qualities, we learn how best to respond to God's gifts and so attain the fullness of grace that he has in store for each one of us. The diversity we see in each other reflects God's own beauty, imagination, and creativity. Made in his image and likeness, each of us reflects certain attributes of God: kindness, humility, beauty, honesty, creativity, intelligence, and more. God dispenses his graces variously in each person in order to express the fullness and perfection of the church. Our personal holiness contributes to the building of God's kingdom on earth. God wants us not only to grow in holiness but also to become a channel of grace for others.

Our own day, the era of the church, is a time of spiritual preparation, a time of waiting for the Lord to come in the power of his Spirit, a time for persistent prayer with and around Mary, like before the first Pentecost. Let us flee to Mary's protection, implore her help, and seek her merciful advocacy.

Reflection and discussion

- What are some of the aspects of whole and mature womanhood expressed through the example and witness of Mary?

- What is the fuller meaning of Christ's virgin birth beyond the physical aspects?

Prayer

Lord God, you raised Mary of Nazareth, the humble maiden of Galilee, to be the royal mother of Israel's Messiah. Prepare my mind and heart to study these sacred texts so that I may better know and love the Blessed Virgin Mary as my own spiritual mother and as queen of all your people. Guide my reading and meditation so that it leads me to prayer and witness, contributing ever more fully to Christ's reign on earth as in heaven. Keep me faithful during these weeks to the challenges that your word offers to me.

SUGGESTIONS FOR FACILITATORS, GROUP SESSION 1

1. If the group is meeting for the first time, or if there are newcomers joining the group, it is helpful to provide name tags.

2. Distribute the books to the members of the group.

3. You may want to ask the participants to introduce themselves and tell the group a bit about themselves.

4. Ask one or more of these introductory questions:
   - What drew you to join this group?
   - What is your biggest fear in beginning this Bible study?
   - How is beginning this study like a "threshold" for you?

5. You may want to pray this prayer as a group:
   Come upon us, Holy Spirit, to enlighten and guide us as we begin this study of Mary, Royal Mother of the Messiah. You inspired the authors of Scripture to reveal your presence throughout the history of salvation. This inspired word has the power to convert our hearts and change our lives. Fill our hearts with desire, trust, and confidence as you shine the light of your truth within us. Motivate us to read the Scriptures and give us a deeper love for God's word each day. Bless us during this session and throughout the coming week with the fire of your love.

6. Read the Introduction aloud, pausing at each question for discussion. Group members may wish to write down the insights of the group as each question is discussed. Encourage several members of the group to respond to each question.

7. Don't feel compelled to finish the complete Introduction during the session. It is better to allow sufficient time to talk about the questions raised than to rush to the end. Group members may read any remaining sections on their own after the group meeting.

8. Instruct group members to read the first six lessons on their own during the six days before the next group meeting. They should write out their own answers to the questions as preparation for next week's group discussion.

9. Fill in the date for each group meeting under "Schedule for Group Study."

10. Conclude by praying aloud together the prayer at the end of the Introduction.

"I will put enmity between you and the woman, and between your offspring and hers; he will strike your head, and you will strike his heel." GENESIS 3:15

New Mother of All Who Live

GENESIS 3:14–20

^{14}*The Lord God said to the serpent,*
  "Because you have done this,
    cursed are you among all animals
    and among all wild creatures;
  upon your belly you shall go,
    and dust you shall eat
    all the days of your life.
^{15}*I will put enmity between you and the woman,*
    and between your offspring and hers;
  he will strike your head,
    and you will strike his heel."
^{16}*To the woman he said,*
  "I will greatly increase your pangs in childbearing;
    in pain you shall bring forth children,
  yet your desire shall be for your husband,
    and he shall rule over you."
^{17}*And to the man he said,*
  "Because you have listened to the voice of your wife,
    and have eaten of the tree
  about which I commanded you,

'You shall not eat of it,'
cursed is the ground because of you;
   in toil you shall eat of it all the days of your life;
[18]*thorns and thistles it shall bring forth for you;*
   and you shall eat the plants of the field.
[19]*By the sweat of your face*
   you shall eat bread
until you return to the ground,
   for out of it you were taken;
you are dust,
   and to dust you shall return."
[20]*The man named his wife Eve, because she was the mother of all who live.*

The opening chapters of the Bible (Gen 1—3), the accounts of creation and sin, form a prologue for the whole history of salvation, just as the closing chapters of Revelation, expressing redemption and new creation, form a finale for the drama of salvation. These first and last chapters of Scripture use highly figurative language to express the reality of God's good creation, followed by the human choice of sin, leading to the world's redemption, and then the glorified creation. Genesis teaches us that God made everything good and formed man and woman as sinless. Yet, human choices and actions, disobedience to the divine will, result in the world's sin and all its consequences.

God formed the man and the woman to equally reflect the divine image, to live in a state of moral goodness, and to share in immortality. Yet, the human choice to sin—a decision the man and woman made together—results in consequences that continue to this day. The woman will bear children with pain; the man will till the stubborn ground with much labor to grow food. Her "desire" for her husband and his "rule" over her describe the tension in their relationship and the conflicts that arise from sin (verses 16–17). The experiences of pain, fear, alienation, and mistrust are foretastes of the ultimate consequence of sin, the return to the dust of the ground (verse 19).

The description of the serpent's punishment (verse 14) concludes with a mysterious oracle: enmity between the serpent and "the woman" and between the serpent's offspring and the woman's offspring (verse 15). This battle between the woman and the serpent continues into the conflict between the offspring (literally "seed") of the serpent and that of the woman. The pronoun "he" refers to the future "seed" of the woman, the one who will strike the head of the serpent, while the serpent and his seed will strike his heel.

Jewish tradition teaches that the one who tempted the woman in the garden is actually Satan, the demonic power through whom sin and death entered the world and continued through future generations. Jewish interpreters also explain that this oracle about the serpent and the woman is a prophecy of the Messiah, the one who would one day rise up and undo the effects of sin. Early Christians continued this tradition and described this oracle as the *Protoevangelium* ("first gospel"), expressing hope for that time when the woman will mortally wound the serpent through her offspring, the Messiah. God does not abandon humanity but offers them a future full of hope. The rest of the Bible will describe how God brings man and woman to a state in which they can again eat of the tree of life and live forever in God's presence.

In the New Testament, Mary is described as the archetypal "woman" of Genesis, whose offspring will conquer the serpent. John begins his gospel with the same words as Genesis, "In the beginning," and describes the story of God's new creation. In this new creation, Jesus addresses his mother as "Woman" (John 2:4). Although the text sounds at first as if Jesus wanted to create some distance from her, the name is a title of honor from the original Paradise. In Genesis, the woman is called "Eve" only once (verse 20), yet she is called "woman" eleven times. Likewise, on the cross, at the very hour when Satan is finally defeated, Jesus again addresses his mother as the "woman" of Genesis, "Woman, here is your son," and to his beloved disciple, "Here is your mother" (John 19:26–27). His dying wish was that all his disciples would take her as their true spiritual mother, the new "mother of all who live."

Mary was honored by the church's early theologians under the titles of the Woman and the new Eve, the woman whose offspring conquers the demonic serpent. St. Irenaeus writes in about AD 180, "The knot of Eve's disobedience was loosed by the obedience of Mary. For what the virgin Eve had bound fast through unbelief, this did the virgin Mary set free through faith." Mary's obedience and faith undoes the knots of Eve's disobedience and unbelief, and she can help her children undo the vices of our lives with her prayers and example. In the name of all humanity, Mary said "yes" to God, where Eve said "no," and by this free act, and by her free suffering with Christ from birth to death, she helps correct the sin of Eve and cooperates with her Son to bring salvation for herself and the whole human race.

Mary is rightly understood as the "woman" of Genesis (Gen 3:15), the "woman" of Cana (John 2:4), the "woman" of Calvary (John 19:26), the "woman" of Galatians (Gal 4:4), and, finally, the "woman" of Revelation (Rev 12:1), the "woman clothed with the sun." This pregnant woman battles the "great red dragon," described as "that ancient serpent, who is called the Devil and Satan, the deceiver of the whole world" (Rev 12:9). This woman is both the mother of the Messiah and a female image of his church. Her offspring conquers Satan and redeems the sin of Adam and Eve through his saving death on the cross. The risen Lord who proclaims, "See, I am making all things new" (Rev 21:5), gives us his mother as a living exemplar of the new creation ushered in by his life, death, and resurrection.

Reflection and discussion

- Why is verse 15 understood by both Jewish and Christian tradition to be a prophecy of the Messiah?

- St. Jerome wrote, "Death came through Eve, but life has come through Mary." How do the Scriptures demonstrate the truth of this teaching?

- Why does Jesus call his mother "Woman" in John's gospel?

- How do the opening chapters of Genesis and the closing chapters of Revelation help me understand the origins and goals of human life?

Prayer

God our Creator, who showed mercy to sinful humanity by promising to strike the head of the serpent through Mary and her offspring, may I honor the mother of your Son as the mother of all the living.

So David and all the house of Israel brought up the ark of the Lord with shouting, and with the sound of the trumpet. 2 SAMUEL 6:15

Ark of the New Covenant

2 SAMUEL 6:2–19 ²*David and all the people with him set out and went from Baale-judah, to bring up from there the ark of God, which is called by the name of the Lord of hosts who is enthroned on the cherubim. ³They carried the ark of God on a new cart, and brought it out of the house of Abinadab, which was on the hill. Uzzah and Ahio, the sons of Abinadab, were driving the new cart ⁴with the ark of God; and Ahio went in front of the ark. ⁵David and all the house of Israel were dancing before the Lord with all their might, with songs and lyres and harps and tambourines and castanets and cymbals.*

⁶When they came to the threshing floor of Nacon, Uzzah reached out his hand to the ark of God and took hold of it, for the oxen shook it. ⁷The anger of the Lord was kindled against Uzzah; and God struck him there because he reached out his hand to the ark; and he died there beside the ark of God. ⁸David was angry because the Lord had burst forth with an outburst upon Uzzah; so that place is called Perez-uzzah, to this day. ⁹David was afraid of the Lord that day; he said, "How can the ark of the Lord come into my care?" ¹⁰So David was unwilling to take the ark of the Lord into his care in the city of David; instead David took it to the house of Obed-edom the Gittite. ¹¹The ark of the Lord remained in the house of Obed-edom the Gittite three months; and the Lord blessed Obed-edom and all his household.

¹²It was told King David, "The Lord has blessed the household of Obed-edom and all that belongs to him, because of the ark of God." So David went and brought up the ark of God from the house of Obed-edom to the city of David with rejoicing; ¹³and when those who bore the ark of the Lord had gone six paces, he sacrificed an ox and a fatling. [14]*David danced before the Lord with all his might; David was girded with a linen ephod.* [15]*So David and all the house of Israel brought up the ark of the Lord with shouting, and with the sound of the trumpet.*

[16]*As the ark of the Lord came into the city of David, Michal daughter of Saul looked out of the window, and saw King David leaping and dancing before the Lord; and she despised him in her heart.*

[17]*They brought in the ark of the Lord, and set it in its place, inside the tent that David had pitched for it; and David offered burnt-offerings and offerings of well-being before the Lord.* [18]*When David had finished offering the burnt-offerings and the offerings of well-being, he blessed the people in the name of the Lord of hosts,* [19]*and distributed food among all the people, the whole multitude of Israel, both men and women, to each a cake of bread, a portion of meat, and a cake of raisins. Then all the people went back to their homes.*

According to God's instructions to Moses, the ark of the covenant was a box-shaped container made of acacia wood and covered inside and out with the purest gold. Two golden cherubim overshadowed the ark, and God was believed to sit invisibly enthroned above the ark on the outstretched wings of the angels (Exod 25:10–16). Inside the ark were preserved sacred remembrances of God's covenant with his people: the tablets of the commandments, a golden urn filled with manna, and the priestly staff of Aaron (Heb 9:4). The portable ark was carried with two golden poles that passed through rings on the ark's sides, moving with the people throughout their wanderings in the wilderness, their settlement in the land, and their battle with enemies. Eventually, the ark of the covenant was brought to Jerusalem by King David and enshrined in God's temple by King Solomon.

The narrative of 2 Samuel 6 describes David's attempt to bring the ark of God up to Jerusalem. He mistakenly transports the ark on a cart of oxen, and when the oxen stumble and the ark is jostled, a man named Uzzah holds the ark to steady it and is struck dead because of the ark's untouchable holiness. David began to fear the Lord's presence and resolved not to bring the ark further. So, the ark remained with Odeb-edom, and the Lord blessed his household (verses 9–11). After three months, David again determined to bring the ark up to the holy city. Amid music, dancing, and sacrificial offerings, the ark was carried up in a festive liturgical procession and placed in the shrine that God's priest-king had prepared.

The ark of the covenant remained in the temple of Jerusalem for four centuries, until the conquest of the city by the Babylonians in 587 BC. 2 Maccabees records that Jeremiah the prophet took the ark and hid it in a cave in the mountains across the Jordan River before the temple was destroyed. The ark has never been found, yet Jeremiah stated, "The place shall remain unknown until God gathers his people together again and shows his mercy. Then the Lord will disclose these things, and the glory of the Lord and the cloud will appear" (2 Maccabees 2:4–8). So, at the time of Jesus, the temple was missing something essential. The Holy of Holies of the temple, which had formerly contained the Lord's ark, had been empty for six centuries. God's people awaited the disclosure of the ark of the new covenant.

The New Testament reveals that Mary is the new ark, the divinely created bearer of the Messiah. As the ark of the old covenant contained the tablets of the Torah, the manna, and Aaron's staff, so the mother of the Lord bears within her virginal womb the incarnate Word, the Bread of Life, and the eternal priest of the new covenant. Luke's account of Mary's annunciation describes the cloud of God's glory that will overshadow Mary, the divine sign awaited by the Jewish people for the revelation of the ark (2 Macc 2:8; Luke 1:35).

Luke's narrative of Mary's journey to the house of Elizabeth contains striking parallels to the account in 2 Samuel 6 of the ark being brought to Jerusalem. Each accounts begin as first David and then Mary "set out and went" to the hill country of Judah (2 Sam 6:2; Luke 1:39). David acknowledges his unworthiness with the words "How can the ark of the Lord come into my care?" (2 Sam 6:9)—words echoed by Elizabeth as Mary approaches her: "Why has this happened to me, that the mother of my Lord comes to me?" (Luke 1:43). The "ark of the Lord" is replaced by "mother of my Lord," and both David and Elizabeth express their unworthiness to be in the presence of the bearer of the Lord. Furthermore, we see David "leaping and dancing" with joy and the people shouting aloud in the presence of the ark (2 Sam 6:14, 16). Likewise, John "leapt for joy" in Elizabeth's womb at the approach of Mary, and Elizabeth shouted with a loud cry (Luke 1:41–42). Finally, the ark remained in the hill country, in the house of Obed-edom, for three months (2 Sam 6:11), the same amount of time Mary remained in the hill country, in the house of Elizabeth (Luke 1:56).

These parallels are not by accident. Luke is taking these events from the life of Mary and looking to the Old Testament to better understand their significance. All of these allusions converge to show how Luke reveals Mary as the ark of the new covenant, the one who bears the divine presence on earth.

A similar revelation of Mary as the ark of the covenant takes place in the book of Revelation. As the scene begins, the visionary sees God's temple in heaven open, and "the ark of the covenant was seen within his temple" amid the sights and sounds of a divine revelation (Rev 11:19). Then as the scene continues (remember, there are no chapter divisions or verse numbers in the original text), a pregnant woman appears in the heavenly temple giving birth to the Messiah (Rev 12:1–2). The true ark of the covenant is no longer on earth but in heaven. For the author of Revelation, the ark of the covenant and the woman clothed with the sun are dual images of the same person, the Blessed Virgin Mary.

Mary becomes for the New Testament what the ark of the covenant was to the Old Testament: God's chosen vessel. Since Mary is the ark of the new covenant, her body is truly the dwelling place of God on earth. She is the divinely created and crafted bearer of the new and eternal covenant between divinity and humanity. As the ark of the old covenant was made of purest gold and kept in the Holy of Holies, where God would descend from heaven to his people, so the ark of the new covenant is pure and completely holy by God's grace. Through her immaculate womb, God descended from heaven to become incarnate in the world. The mystery of Mary's identity as the new ark illuminates the even more wondrous mystery of Jesus as the divine presence on earth.

Reflection and discussion

- Why was Uzzah struck dead when he touched the ark of the covenant? What is the lesson of this event for David and the Israelite people?

- Why did God prepare such a pure and sinless vessel for the incarnation of his Son in the world?

- What is most significant for me about Mary's title as Ark of the New Covenant?

Prayer

God of the covenant, who instructed Moses to craft the ark of the covenant as the bearer of your presence with your people, give me the desire to honor Mary as the bearer of your incarnate presence in the world.

The king rose to meet her, and bowed down to her; then he sat on his throne, and had a throne brought for the king's mother, and she sat on his right. 1 KINGS 2:19

Queen Mother of God's Kingdom

1 KINGS 2:12–20 ¹²*So Solomon sat on the throne of his father David; and his kingdom was firmly established.*

¹³*Then Adonijah son of Haggith came to Bathsheba, Solomon's mother. She asked, "Do you come peaceably?" He said, "Peaceably." ¹⁴Then he said, "May I have a word with you?" She said, "Go on." ¹⁵He said, "You know that the kingdom was mine, and that all Israel expected me to reign; however, the kingdom has turned about and become my brother's, for it was his from the Lord. ¹⁶And now I have one request to make of you; do not refuse me." She said to him, "Go on." ¹⁷He said, "Please ask King Solomon—he will not refuse you—to give me Abishag the Shunammite as my wife." ¹⁸Bathsheba said, "Very well; I will speak to the king on your behalf."*

¹⁹*So Bathsheba went to King Solomon, to speak to him on behalf of Adonijah. The king rose to meet her, and bowed down to her; then he sat on his throne, and had a throne brought for the king's mother, and she sat on his right. ²⁰Then she said, "I have one small request to make of you; do not refuse me." And the king said to her, "Make your request, my mother; for I will not refuse you."*

The mother of a ruling monarch held an important position in many kingdoms of the Ancient Near East, influencing political, military, economic, and cultic affairs in the royal court. It was the king's mother who ruled as queen, not the king's wife. We see this in Hittite, Ugaritic, Egyptian, and

Assyrian kingdoms, as well as in ancient Israel. The importance of the king's mother may seem odd until we recall that most kings in the Ancient Near East practiced polygamy and had large harems. While kings may have had many wives, they each had only one mother, and the queenship was given to her.

This role of the queen mother is what we find in the Old Testament texts, where the king's mother was given preeminence over all the women in the kingdom of Judah. She was given the title "Great Lady" (*Gebirah*, in Hebrew), reigning as queen in her son's kingdom. In the succession narratives of 1 and 2 Kings, in which all the kings in the lineage of King David are introduced in dynastic succession, the mother of the king is consistently announced, highlighting the queen mother's important place alongside the king. She represented the king's continuity with the past, the blood link with the previous king, through which God's dynastic promise to David was fulfilled.

The queen mother was not simply an honorary position. She had real royal authority, participating in her son's reign. We see this influence when we compare Bathsheba's role when she was the wife of King David to her role when she became the queen mother of King Solomon. When she wants to enter the royal chamber of her husband David, she bows before him and pays him homage (1 Kings 1:16), and as she leaves she honors the king, saying, "May my lord King David live forever!" (1 Kings 1:31). In the next chapter, David has died and Bathsheba's son Solomon has assumed the throne, making her the king's mother. When she enters the royal chamber as the queen mother, "the king rose to meet her, and bowed down to her" (1 Kings 2:19). Then Solomon had "a throne brought in for the king's mother," symbolizing her royal position. Even more remarkable is the place where Solomon places his mother's throne: at his right hand, the position of authority and supreme honor. Nowhere else in the Old Testament does a king offer such respect to anyone as Solomon offers the *Gebirah*, the "Great Lady" of Israel.

The influence of the queen mother is seen in the intercessory role she played in ancient Israel. She served as an advocate, taking petitions from the people and presenting them to the king. Her new intercessory power is immediately recognized when Adonijah asks Bathsheba to bring a petition of his to the king. Adonijah expresses great confidence in her intercessory role, saying, "Please ask King Solomon—he will not refuse you" (1 Kings 2:17). Bathsheba agrees and then goes to the king, in whose presence she is welcomed with great dignity. Bathsheba tells Solomon she has a small request to bring to him. Solomon responds by saying, "Make your request, my mother; for I will not refuse you" (1 Kings 2:20). Indeed, Solomon's words reveal the king's commitment to the queen mother's petitions.

The queen mother held an official position in the royal court, sharing in the shepherding responsibilities of the king and serving as a counselor for the king and as an advocate for the people. For example, in Proverbs, a queen mother gives wise counsel to her son about how to serve the poor, rule the people with justice, avoid too much alcohol, and choose a good wife (Prov 31:1–9). At the time of the conquest by Babylon, she is described by Jeremiah as having a throne and a crown which she will lose in exile (Jer 13:18). The prophecy portrays the queen mother (*gebirah*) as participating in the king's reign and sharing in the king's mission of shepherding the people of Judah, a flock that is about to be taken away from them: "Where is the flock that was given you, your beautiful flock?" (Jer 13:20).

Significantly, 2 Kings names the queen mother among the members of the royal court whom King Jehoiachin surrenders to the king of Babylon. The queen mother is the first of the king's royal court listed as being given over to Babylon to go into exile (2 Kings 24:12, 15). She is mentioned before "the king's wives" and before the ministers, dignitaries, and officers. The *gebirah* is clearly second only to the king in the list of prominent officials brought into captivity. All of these details emphasize that, after the monarch himself, the queen mother has the place of highest honor in the kingdom.

Because Mary is the mother of the Messiah, the new and final King of the everlasting lineage of David, she is the queen mother of his reign. In the kingdom of God, brought to its fullness in Jesus Christ, she is the royal mother, participating in the reign of her Son and serving as advocate of the people, interceding for them and bringing their petitions to her Son. No one who flees to her protection, implores her help, or seeks her intercession is left unaided.

Reflection and discussion

- What are some of the roles of the queen mother within the royal line of King David?

- In what ways does Mary demonstrate her role as royal advocate and intercessor in the kingdom of her Son?

- How do I honor Mary as the queen mother, the great Lady, of God's reign among his people?

Prayer

Hail holy Queen, mother of mercy, we cry to you as the banished children of Eve. Turn your compassionate gaze upon us in our exile. Let us trust in you with confidence as our advocate before the throne of your Son Jesus.

Therefore he shall give them up until the time when she who is in labor has brought forth; then the rest of his kindred shall return to the people of Israel. MICAH 5:3

Prophecies of the New Royal Mother

ISAIAH 7:10–14 *¹⁰Again the Lord spoke to Ahaz, saying, ¹¹Ask a sign of the Lord your God; let it be deep as Sheol or high as heaven. ¹²But Ahaz said, I will not ask, and I will not put the Lord to the test. ¹³Then Isaiah said: "Hear then, O house of David! Is it too little for you to weary mortals, that you weary my God also? ¹⁴Therefore the Lord himself will give you a sign. Look, the young woman is with child and shall bear a son, and shall name him Immanuel.*

MICAH 5:2–5
²But you, O Bethlehem of Ephrathah,
*   who are one of the little clans of Judah,*
from you shall come forth for me
*   one who is to rule in Israel,*
whose origin is from of old,
*   from ancient days.*
³Therefore he shall give them up until the time
*   when she who is in labor has brought forth;*
then the rest of his kindred shall return
*   to the people of Israel.*
⁴And he shall stand and feed his flock in the strength of the Lord,
*   in the majesty of the name of the Lord his God.*

And they shall live secure, for now he shall be great
   to the ends of the earth;
⁵and he shall be the one of peace.

The Immanuel prophecies of Isaiah emphasize the important role of the queen mother in the Davidic lineage, the "house of David." Under threat of invasion, Ahaz the king of Judah fears that the dynasty of David could be coming to an end, and God's faithfulness to the Davidic dynasty is called into question (2 Sam 7:11–14). Isaiah is sent by God to encourage the king to stand firm in the threat and be confident in God's continuing faithfulness to David's line.

As a confirmation of God's protection of the house of David, the prophet gives an assuring sign from the Lord: "Look, the young woman (*almah*, in Hebrew) is with child and shall bear a son, and shall name him Immanuel" (Isa 7:14). The Hebrew word means "a marriageable maiden." In the Septuagint Greek text, the version more familiar to the early Christians, the word is *parthenos*, meaning "virgin." The "child" represents an heir to the throne in the lineage of David, a guarantee that the succession will continue as God has promised.

The child's name, *Immanuel* (God with us), expresses God's promise to be "with" the successors of David in a special way. God will still be with his people even though the house of David appears to be crumbling in the crisis. This child is also associated with the other Immanuel prophecies of Isaiah 9:2–7 (a child who will bring about "endless peace for the throne of David and his kingdom") and Isaiah 11 (a royal son upon whom "the spirit of the Lord shall rest," who will unify all people and whom all nations will seek). The young woman conceiving this royal son is the mother of the king in the lineage of David, the queen mother who will participate in the rule of her son and serve as advocate of his people.

The prophecy of Micah, a contemporary of Isaiah, also speaks of a future ruler who would bring salvation from threatening enemies. Like Isaiah, he introduces this coming king by speaking of the royal mother who would give birth to a king of the lineage of David (verses 2–3). The origin of this future king is "from of old, from ancient days," that is, his reign is rooted in God's ancient covenant with David, and he will come forth from Bethlehem, where David was born and raised. Like David, the shepherd king, the coming ruler will "feed his flock" and bring security to this people (verses 4–5).

Because these prophecies did not find satisfactory fulfillment in the generations immediately following King Ahaz in the eighth century before Christ, their high ideals began to express the messianic hope for a future age. Matthew quotes these texts in the infancy narrative of his gospel to express the continuity between God's working throughout the tradition of Israel and God's new work in the coming of the Messiah. We see in these passages that when the prophets began to speak of the future Messiah, they spoke also of the future queen mother.

We can imagine Jewish women in the first century wondering who would be the mother of the long-awaited Messiah, the new queen mother of God's people. Matthew's gospel makes clear that Isaiah's prophecy of the queen mother and her son is fulfilled in Mary and her royal Son Jesus: "All this took place to fulfill what had been spoken by the Lord through the prophet: 'Look, the virgin shall conceive and bear a son, and they shall name him Emmanuel,' which means, 'God is with us'" (Matt 1:22–23). If Jesus is the Messiah, then Mary his mother is the new queen, the mother of Emmanuel (an alternate spelling of Immanuel). She is the virgin who will bear a son who is "God with us."

Bethlehem was a tiny village a short distance south of Jerusalem, almost unnoticed and forgotten alongside the great city. Micah calls Bethlehem "one of the little clans of Judah"; but Matthew amends the text and calls Bethlehem "by no means least among the rulers of Judah" (Matt 2:6). Throughout salvation history, God has done wondrous things with those people and places who are the smallest, the least likely, and the unexpected. The announcement that the Messiah of the world is the baby lying in a manger beside his young mother in Bethlehem is the fullest expression of the biblical theme that God works in these inconspicuous ways.

Reflection and discussion

- Why is it fitting that Christians give Mary the honor due to her as the queen of Christ's kingdom?

- What is the difference between worshiping Jesus Christ and giving honor to his mother Mary?

- In what challenges must I realize that Jesus is "God with us" and that Mary is the mother of Emmanuel?

Prayer

O come Emmanuel, ransom your captive and exiled people. Feed your flock and give us peace to the ends of the earth. Grant me the hope and confident trust of your mother Mary, queen of the kingdom of God.

**A voice is heard in Ramah, lamentation and bitter weeping.
Rachel is weeping for her children; she refuses to be
comforted for her children, because they are no more.**
JEREMIAH 31:15

The Mother Weeping
for Her Children

GENESIS 35:16–20 ¹⁶*Then they journeyed from Bethel; and when they were still
some distance from Ephrath, Rachel was in childbirth, and she had a difficult labor.
*¹⁷*When she was in her difficult labor, the midwife said to her, "Do not be afraid;
for now you will have another son." *¹⁸*As her soul was departing (for she died), she
named him Ben-oni; but his father called him Benjamin. *¹⁹*So Rachel died, and she
was buried on the way to Ephrath (that is, Bethlehem), *²⁰*and Jacob set up a pillar at
her grave; it is the pillar of Rachel's tomb, which is there to this day.*

JEREMIAH 31:15–17
    ¹⁵*Thus says the Lord:*
    A voice is heard in Ramah,
        lamentation and bitter weeping.
    Rachel is weeping for her children;
        she refuses to be comforted for her children,
        because they are no more.
    ¹⁶*Thus says the Lord:*
    Keep your voice from weeping,
        and your eyes from tears;

for there is a reward for your work, says the Lord:
   they shall come back from the land of the enemy;
¹⁷*there is hope for your future, says the Lord:*
   your children shall come back to their own country.

R achel was the beloved wife of Jacob, the father of the twelve tribes of Israel. She was graceful and beautiful, and Jacob truly loved her. Yet, Rachel's life was filled with intense suffering. When delivering Benjamin, the twelfth son of Jacob, she died in childbirth (Gen 35:16–18). Rachel is not buried in the family tomb with the other matriarchs of Israel; instead, she is buried on the road near Bethlehem in a tomb that is known "to this day" (Gen 35:19–20).

Rachel is the biological mother of Joseph and Benjamin, but she is considered the mother of all Israel. She suffers with all her children and cries tears of sorrow for them centuries after her own death and burial (Jer 31:15). She is "weeping for her children" who have been killed or driven from the land into exile; "she refuses to be comforted" as they pass by her tomb on their way to Babylon. Yet, her mournful intercession moves the heart of God, for God tells Rachel to weep no more because her work will be rewarded by the return of her children to their own land (Jer 31:16–17).

In the Jewish tradition, Rachel is considered as the most powerful intercessor on behalf of Israel before God. Through the centuries, Jews have visited Rachel's tomb to light candles and plead for her prayers. Because of the depths of her motherly sorrow, Rachel's intercession with God succeeds when other interventions fail. For this reason, she is regarded in a special way as the sorrowful mother of all Israel, the woman who prays for and intercedes on behalf of her children.

In the New Testament, Rachel's sorrowful mediation is invoked as all the infant children are killed by Herod (Matt 2:16–18). This massacre occurs in the vicinity of Rachel's tomb, in Bethlehem and the surrounding region. As the mother of Israel, Rachel is again lamenting for the suffering of her descendants. She who wept from her grave near Bethlehem at the time of Israel's captivity now weeps at another time of crisis in the life of God's people. Though long dead, Rachel is not oblivious to the suffering of her children on earth.

As the suffering mothers and merciful intercessors for God's people, Rachel and Mary are counterparts of each other. Rachel's sorrow for her exiled and deceased children expresses the suffering of Mary in relationship to her Son, Israel's Messiah. Mary, in Matthew's gospel, as the suffering mother of her persecuted child driven into exile, is a new Rachel. She weeps for her Son throughout his life and becomes the sorrowful mother for all her children in his church.

In John's gospel, Jesus himself compared his passion and crucifixion to the sorrow of a woman in childbirth (John 16:21–22). Just as Rachel gave birth to her second-born son, Benjamin, through suffering and dying in childbirth, so Mary, the mother of the crucified Messiah, gives birth spiritually to her second son, "the beloved disciple," through her maternal suffering at Golgotha. Since the beloved disciple represents all disciples, Mary becomes the mother of Christ's church just as Rachel is the mother of all Israel.

Finally, John's vision of the woman clothed with the sun, with the moon under her feet, and on her head a crown of twelve stars (Rev 12:1–3) is based on the dream of Rachel's son Joseph. In his dream, the sun, moon, and stars symbolize Jacob, Rachel, and their twelve sons (Gen 37:9–10). Mary as the heavenly mother of the Messiah fulfills Joseph's dream and is exalted by all her ancestors. As the heavenly woman cries out in her birth pangs, we call to mind the anguished childbirth of her ancestor Rachel. The dragon is angry with the heavenly mother and makes war on the rest of her children. As Rachel was regarded as the mother of all God's persecuted children in the Old Testament, so the heavenly woman of Revelation is mother of all who believe in Jesus but are persecuted by the forces of evil.

Mary is the new Rachel, the Mother of Sorrows (*Mater Dolorosa*). She united herself with the sacrifice of her Son and made her own maternal contribution to the work of salvation. Through his sorrowful passion and her own motherly suffering, like the pangs of labor, a new humanity was born. Despite her exalted status as the new Eve, the ark of the new covenant, and the new queen mother, Mary is a human woman who knows what it is to endure excruciating pain and be filled with sorrow.

As the new Rachel, Mary is a powerful intercessor for her children. If God listens to the weeping of Rachel, the mother of his beloved children of Israel, then God must surely listen to the weeping of Mary, the sorrowful mother of his Son and of all his disciples, especially those suffering exile, persecution, and injustice in the world.

Reflection and discussion

- How does the story of Rachel illustrate that out of death is born new life?

- Which comparison between Rachel and Mary is most striking to me?

- Why is Mary such a powerful intercessor for those who suffer?

Prayer

Mother of Sorrows, we take refuge in your mercy because God listens to your prayers for your children in distress. Turn your compassionate gaze upon us as we stand with you at the foot of the cross.

Then Uzziah said to her, "O daughter, you are blessed by the Most High God above all other women on earth."
JUDITH 13:18

The Highest Honor of Our Race

JUDITH 13:18–20 ¹⁸*Then Uzziah said to her, "O daughter, you are blessed by the Most High God above all other women on earth; and blessed be the Lord God, who created the heavens and the earth, who has guided you to cut off the head of the leader of our enemies.* ¹⁹*Your praise will never depart from the hearts of those who remember the power of God.* ²⁰*May God grant this to be a perpetual honor to you, and may he reward you with blessings, because you risked your own life when our nation was brought low, and you averted our ruin, walking in the straight path before our God." And all the people said, "Amen. Amen."*

15:8–13 ⁸*Then the high priest Joakim and the elders of the Israelites who lived in Jerusalem came to witness the good things that the Lord had done for Israel, and to see Judith and to wish her well.* ⁹*When they met her, they all blessed her with one accord and said to her, "You are the glory of Jerusalem, you are the great boast of Israel, you are the great pride of our nation!* ¹⁰*You have done all this with your own hand; you have done great good to Israel, and God is well pleased with it. May the Almighty Lord bless you forever!" And all the people said, "Amen."*

¹¹*All the people plundered the camp for thirty days. They gave Judith the tent of Holofernes and all his silver dinnerware, his beds, his bowls, and all his furniture. She took them and loaded her mules and hitched up her carts and piled the things on them.*

[12]All the women of Israel gathered to see her, and blessed her, and some of them performed a dance in her honor. She took ivy-wreathed wands in her hands and distributed them to the women who were with her; [13]and she and those who were with her crowned themselves with olive wreaths. She went before all the people in the dance, leading all the women, while all the men of Israel followed, bearing their arms and wearing garlands and singing hymns.

From the point of view of Christianity, the Old Testament anticipates, announces, and points to the New Testament. The two relate to each other like promise and fulfillment. Looking from the New Testament back into the Old Testament, we recognize a number of women of importance who prefigure Mary in some aspects of their personality, vocation, and destiny. As we have seen, Mary is the new Eve, the new queen mother of Israel, and the new Rachel. The stories of many other women of the Old Testament anticipate and intuit the life of Mary, the royal mother of the Messiah.

Sarah, the beautiful wife of Abraham, responds faithfully to God's initiatives and brings God's promises to fruition. Because she is filled with faith, God works through her to bear a son despite her barrenness. She became the mother of Isaac and then the mother of all believers. Sarah's barrenness is ended with the Lord saying to Abraham, "Is anything too wonderful for the Lord?" (Gen 18:14). Mary, too, conceives because of her faith and is told by the angel that "nothing will be impossible with God." God says of Sarah, "She shall give rise to nations" (Gen 17:16), and Mary becomes the mother of all people.

Miriam, the sister of Moses the lawgiver and Aaron the priest of the old covenant, is present with her brothers at the tent of meeting. Mary, the mother of Jesus, the eternal law giver and high priest, is herself the ark of the new covenant who bears the presence of God. Miriam is considered a prophet of Israel and sings the victory song of God's deliverance at the exodus (Exodus 15:20–21). Mary, too, sings of God's triumph over the proud and mighty ones in her Magnificat.

Deborah is a remarkable leader of Israel who has the gifts of prophecy and wisdom. She is Barak's active partner in Israel's conquest of the Canaanites. Her decisions result in victory for Israel at the hands of another courageous woman, Jael. In her victory song, Deborah shows total confidence in God and attributes the victory to God's power (Judg 5). Likewise, Mary displays the gift of wisdom and sings of the power of God over Israel's enemies. She is an active partner with Christ in the victory over evil and sin, and her song proclaims the greatness of the Lord. In Deborah's victory song, Jael is praised: "Most blessed of women be Jael," while Mary is praised by Elizabeth: "Blessed are you among women."

Queen Esther intercedes with the king of Persia and risks her life to save her people from a decree of death. Likewise, Mary continually intercedes with her royal Son, Jesus Christ, and cooperates in his redemptive mission to save humanity from the decree of eternal death.

The noble mother of the Maccabees watches and supports her seven sons as they are tortured and murdered because of their fidelity to the covenant (2 Macc 7). When the persecutor calls upon her to intervene with her last son, to urge him to accept offers of wealth and power to save his life, the mother appeals to her son, exhorting him to accept death, so that in God's mercy she may have all her sons restored to life in the resurrection. Likewise, Mary watches and supports her Son in his torturous death on the cross. As he overcomes the temptations that would end his redemptive mission, Mary stands firm with courage, weeps with tears of sorrow, and trusts in God's promise of resurrection by which she would receive her Son in his glorified life.

Finally, the valiant Judith is a woman of courage, beauty, and selfless sacrifice for her people. Following the prescriptions of the Torah and observing the feasts of Israel, she represents the entire faithful people of Israel and is held in high repute by all. In her heroic action, she battles Holofernes, the leader of Israel's enemy, triumphing over him by cutting off his head (verse 18), intimating the enmity between the serpent and the "woman" of Genesis 3:15.

Like her ancestor Judith, Mary places her absolute trust in God and is exemplary in her prayer, observes the law's ritual prescriptions, and celebrates Israel's feasts. The angelic salutation to Mary echoes the blessing of Judith: "O daughter, you are blessed by the Most High God above all other women on earth" (Jdt 13:18). In the song and response of the Christian tradition, the praise of Judith is celebrated also in Mary: "You are the glory of Jerusalem, you are the great boast of Israel, you are the great pride of our nation!" (Jdt 15:9). In liturgical procession, God's people gather to honor Mary as they do for Judith, crowned with wreaths, wearing garlands, honoring her with dance, and singing hymns (Jdt 15:12–13).

Reflection and discussion

- The women of Israel were heroes and mentors of Mary, the mother of Jesus. Which of these women might she have particularly admired?

- How do the heroic qualities of Judith anticipate the virtues of Mary?

- What are some ways that you have honored Mary as the queen mother of Christ?

Prayer

Royal Mother Mary, the great pride of our church, you are blessed by the Most High God above all other women on earth. May we increase our devotion as we honor you with procession, prayer, and praise.

SUGGESTIONS FOR FACILITATORS, GROUP SESSION 2

1. If there are newcomers who were not present for the first group session, introduce them now.

2. You may want to pray this prayer as a group:

   Lord God of Israel, you have lifted up your daughter Mary to be the new mother of all the living, the ark of the new covenant, the mother of the Messiah, the mother of Emmanuel, the mother of sorrows, and the great pride of your people. Grant us the hope and confident trust of Mary, who became the bearer of your incarnate presence in the world. May we sing her praises as we honor her as the queen of your kingdom and our advocate before the throne of your Son, Jesus Christ.

3. Ask one or both of the following questions:
   - What was your biggest challenge in Bible study over this past week?
   - What did you learn about yourself this week?

4. Discuss lessons 1 through 6 together. Assuming that group members have read the Scripture and commentary during the week, there is no need to read it aloud. As you review each lesson, you might want to briefly summarize the Scripture passages of each lesson and ask the group what stands out most clearly from the commentary.

5. Choose one or more of the questions for reflection and discussion from each lesson to talk over as a group. You may want to ask group members which question was most challenging or helpful to them as you review each lesson.

6. Keep the discussion moving, but don't rush the discussion in order to complete more questions. Allow time for the questions that provoke the most discussion.

7. Instruct group members to complete lessons 7 through 12 on their own during the six days before the next group meeting. They should write out their own answers to the questions as preparation for next week's group discussion.

8. Conclude by praying aloud together the prayer at the end of lesson 6 or any other prayer you choose.

Salmon the father of Boaz by Rahab, and Boaz the father of Obed by Ruth, and Obed the father of Jesse, and Jesse the father of King David.
MATTHEW 1:5–6

The Ancestors and Mother of the Messiah

MATTHEW 1:1–16 ¹*An account of the genealogy of Jesus the Messiah, the son of David, the son of Abraham.*

²*Abraham was the father of Isaac, and Isaac the father of Jacob, and Jacob the father of Judah and his brothers,* ³*and Judah the father of Perez and Zerah by Tamar, and Perez the father of Hezron, and Hezron the father of Aram,* ⁴*and Aram the father of Aminadab, and Aminadab the father of Nahshon, and Nahshon the father of Salmon,* ⁵*and Salmon the father of Boaz by Rahab, and Boaz the father of Obed by Ruth, and Obed the father of Jesse,* ⁶*and Jesse the father of King David.*

And David was the father of Solomon by the wife of Uriah, ⁷*and Solomon the father of Rehoboam, and Rehoboam the father of Abijah, and Abijah the father of Asaph,* ⁸*and Asaph the father of Jehoshaphat, and Jehoshaphat the father of Joram, and Joram the father of Uzziah,* ⁹*and Uzziah the father of Jotham, and Jotham the father of Ahaz, and Ahaz the father of Hezekiah,* ¹⁰*and Hezekiah the father of Manasseh, and Manasseh the father of Amos, and Amos the father of Josiah,* ¹¹*and Josiah the father of Jechoniah and his brothers, at the time of the deportation to Babylon.*

¹²*And after the deportation to Babylon: Jechoniah was the father of Salathiel, and Salathiel the father of Zerubbabel,* ¹³*and Zerubbabel the father of Abiud, and Abiud the father of Eliakim, and Eliakim the father of Azor,* ¹⁴*and Azor the father of Zadok, and Zadok the father of Achim, and Achim the father of Eliud,* ¹⁵*and Eliud the father of Eleazar, and Eleazar the father of Matthan, and Matthan the father of*

Jacob, ¹⁶and Jacob the father of Joseph the husband of Mary, of whom Jesus was born, who is called the Messiah.

Matthew begins his gospel by linking the narrative of Jesus with the history of his ancestors and showing him to be the achievement of Israel's highest hopes. This genealogy reminds us explicitly that our identity in Jesus is rooted in the memory of our ancestors in the Old Testament. The first verse highlights three titles of Jesus that will be developed throughout the gospel. "Messiah" proclaims him as the anointed king who will fulfill Israel's longing for a deliverer to bring salvation. "Son of David" is a messianic title announcing Jesus as a royal descendant from the lineage of King David. The title indicates that Jesus would complete the promises God made to David that his dynasty and his kingdom would last forever (2 Sam 7:12, 16). "Son of Abraham" links Jesus with the beginnings of God's covenant with Israel, promising that in the descendants of Abraham all the nations of the earth would gain blessing (Gen 22:18).

It is unusual for women to be listed in an Israelite genealogy, yet this list of ancestors contains four women from the Old Testament and culminates in "Mary, of whom Jesus was born" (verse 16). These four women, along with Mary, are all motherly predecessors to the kings of David's royal lineage, and each of them play a crucial role in God's plan to bring Israel to its messianic fulfillment. Yet, these women are not the great matriarchs and female prophets of Israel's history, and they seem unlikely choices to be included in the messianic lineage.

Tamar (verse 3), a Canaanite, was left childless after the death of her spouses. She disguised herself as a prostitute and seduced her father-in-law Judah in order to bear a child. Rahab (verse 5), another Canaanite, was a genuine prostitute who sheltered the spies of Israel when they came to Jericho. Ruth, a Moabite, journeyed to Judah after the death of her Israelite husband and married Boaz in Bethlehem. Bathsheba, "the wife of Uriah" (verse 6), a Hittite, became the wife of King David after he shamefully impregnated her and arranged her husband's death.

Each of these women was considered an outsider, a foreigner. Their presence in the genealogy of Jesus foreshadows his messianic mission, which invited Gentiles as well as Jews into the kingdom of God. Each also had an unusual marital or sexual history that could be seen as scandalous or scornful and that placed her life in peril. Their inclusion along with a host of corrupt and scandalous men in the genealogy prepares the reader for the ministry of Jesus in which sinners and prostitutes enter the kingdom. All of these women and men give us a preview of that peculiar collection of humble, marginalized, and endangered people who will encounter Jesus and experience the salvation of his kingdom. Indeed, the universal gospel of Jesus Christ welcomes all and breaks down the barriers between Jew and Gentile, male and female, sinner and saint.

Mary (verse 16) is the final woman in the genealogy. Like the women who preceded her, her marital situation was highly unusual and shocking to outsiders. Yet, all five of these women, despite their situations, played an important role in continuing the lineage of the Messiah. Tamar continued the family line of Judah's son through her initiative and loyalty despite grave personal danger. Rahab made it possible for the Israelites to possess the promised land while securing safety for her whole household. Ruth struggled for survival and gave birth to the grandfather of King David. Bathsheba guaranteed that her son Solomon succeeded David and was the foundational queen mother in the long lineage of David. Finally, Mary's response to God's unanticipated call enabled her to become God's greatest instrument and to bring the lineage of the Messiah to its completion. Each of these women, in distressed conditions, dreamed of a future and acted to bring it about, thus partnering with God's redemptive work.

The names of Joseph, Mary, and Jesus break the steady rhythm of the genealogical pattern. The shift indicates that Joseph did not father Jesus, according to human descent, and emphasizes that Jesus was born of Mary. The virginal conception of Jesus introduces something radically new as the messianic age dawns. Though adopted by Joseph into David's royal line, Jesus is begotten of God through Mary and begins the new era of God's saving plan.

Reflection and discussion

- Which women among my ancestors helped shape my identity and self-understanding?

- What meaning do I find for myself in Matthew's inclusion of these particular women in Jesus' genealogy?

- How might these female ancestors have helped Mary form her own identity as mother of Israel's Messiah?

Prayer

God of our ancestors, you prepared the world for the coming of the Messiah through the legacy of these women and men. Help me to honor the heritage of my forebears and make my life a new witness in your saving plan for the world.

"Joseph, son of David, do not be afraid to take Mary as your wife, for the child conceived in her is from the Holy Spirit."
MATTHEW 1:20

Mary Gives Birth to Emmanuel

MATTHEW 1:18–25 ¹⁸*Now the birth of Jesus the Messiah took place in this way. When his mother Mary had been engaged to Joseph, but before they lived together, she was found to be with child from the Holy Spirit.* ¹⁹*Her husband Joseph, being a righteous man and unwilling to expose her to public disgrace, planned to dismiss her quietly.* ²⁰*But just when he had resolved to do this, an angel of the Lord appeared to him in a dream and said, "Joseph, son of David, do not be afraid to take Mary as your wife, for the child conceived in her is from the Holy Spirit.* ²¹*She will bear a son, and you are to name him Jesus, for he will save his people from their sins."* ²²*All this took place to fulfill what had been spoken by the Lord through the prophet:*

²³*"Look, the virgin shall conceive and bear a son,*
and they shall name him Emmanuel,"

which means, "God is with us." ²⁴*When Joseph awoke from sleep, he did as the angel of the Lord commanded him; he took her as his wife,* ²⁵*but had no marital relations with her until she had borne a son; and he named him Jesus.*

Matthew conveys the identity of Jesus as he narrates the story of the Messiah's birth. Through the lineage of Joseph and his legal paternity, Jesus is Son of David. Through the Holy Spirit and the virginal maternity of Mary, he is Son of God. The obedient and willing responses of both Joseph and Mary are necessary for the coming of the Savior.

The couple was between the two states of Jewish marriage. They had completed the first stage, the formal exchange of consent, made at the home of the bride's father. They were preparing for the second stage, made about a year later: the solemn transfer of the bride to the house of the groom. During this time, Joseph was painstakingly building a house and making sure all was right for him and his new family. The betrothal of Mary and Joseph was a legally contracted marriage, completed "before they lived together" (verse 18). Joseph was already called "her husband" (verse 19), and Mary was already Joseph's "wife" (verse 20).

Joseph became aware of Mary's pregnancy before God revealed to him its meaning and cause. Joseph knew that Mary was holy and honorable, yet he also knew that the pregnancy could only be the result of either willing or forced relations with another man. According to the law given in Deuteronomy, Joseph could have exposed Mary to the humiliation of a public procedure, but he chose to quietly divorce her, without accusation, trial, punishment, and shame.

The divine revelation given in his dream cut short one agonizing choice and presented him with another: the choice to cooperate with the incredible workings of God. His choice to do "as the angel of the Lord commanded him" (verse 24) caught him up in the cosmic drama wherein heaven and earth met in the child of Mary's womb.

The conception of the child in Mary's womb was revealed to be "from the Holy Spirit" (verses 18, 20). In the Old Testament, the Spirit of God was linked with God's creating power, the inspired words of the prophets, and God's creation anew in the last days. The work of the Holy Spirit in the womb of Mary both continued and brought to a climax God's work throughout Israel's history.

The text of the prophet Isaiah, "Look, the virgin shall conceive and bear a son, and they shall name him Emmanuel" (verse 23), was an oracle of hope given originally to the house of David in the eighth century before Christ. The dynasty of David was once again in jeopardy because of invading armies. In that bleak situation, Isaiah prophesied a divine sign of assurance, a sign guaranteeing God's continual faithfulness to David's lineage. The prophecy spoke of the approaching birth of a king, born from the dynasty of David. His birth and reign would bring restoration to the people and would be a sign that God is truly with his people.

The mother of the future king is called a young maiden in the Hebrew text, but the Greek text, the version more familiar to the early Christians, specified that the maiden was a "virgin." In the Old Testament, Israel is often referred to as a young woman and sometimes specifically as a virgin. The later Jewish period understood Isaiah's words as a messianic prophecy, proposing that virgin Israel would give birth to the Messiah.

Matthew understood that this ancient prophecy found its fuller meaning in the light of Jesus. The text fortified the faith of the early church in the messianic identity of Jesus and his virginal conception. Through the ancient text, the evangelist proclaims that Jesus is the long-awaited savior, that he was born of Mary the virgin, and that through him God is with his people in a completely new way. Mary represents virgin Israel, implying that God's people cannot bring forth the Messiah from their own human history but only through the direct intervention of God. In these ways, Matthew's citation of Isaiah's text stresses the continuity between God's saving work throughout the ancient tradition and God's new work of salvation in the Messiah's coming.

Reflection and discussion

- What are some of the emotions felt by women when they discover they are pregnant? What mixture of feelings might Mary have felt in these moments?

- What is the meaning and significance in God's plan that Mary was a virgin? What does Mary's virginity tell us about Jesus?

- What do I find to be most noble about Joseph, the spouse of Mary?

- How has this passage challenged me to greater trust? What can I do to demonstrate my confidence in God to those around me?

Prayer

God our help in ages past, you bring new hope to your people through the pregnancy of women and the birth of children. Give me a spirit of trusting confidence in your presence and give me faith in Jesus, our Emmanuel.

On entering the house, they saw the child with Mary his mother; and they knelt down and paid him homage. Then, opening their treasure-chests, they offered him gifts of gold, frankincense, and myrrh. MATTHEW 2:11

Magi Pay Homage to the Son of Mary

MATTHEW 2:1–12 ¹*In the time of King Herod, after Jesus was born in Bethlehem of Judea, wise men from the East came to Jerusalem,* ²*asking, "Where is the child who has been born king of the Jews? For we observed his star at its rising, and have come to pay him homage."* ³*When King Herod heard this, he was frightened, and all Jerusalem with him;* ⁴*and calling together all the chief priests and scribes of the people, he inquired of them where the Messiah was to be born.* ⁵*They told him, "In Bethlehem of Judea; for so it has been written by the prophet:*

⁶*'And you, Bethlehem, in the land of Judah,*

are by no means least among the rulers of Judah;

for from you shall come a ruler

who is to shepherd my people Israel.'"

⁷*Then Herod secretly called for the wise men and learned from them the exact time when the star had appeared.* ⁸*Then he sent them to Bethlehem, saying, "Go and search diligently for the child; and when you have found him, bring me word so that I may also go and pay him homage."* ⁹*When they had heard the king, they set out; and there, ahead of them, went the star that they had seen at its rising, until it stopped over the place where the child was.* ¹⁰*When they saw that the star had stopped, they were overwhelmed with joy.* ¹¹*On entering the house, they saw the child with Mary his mother; and they knelt down and paid him homage. Then, opening their treasure-chests, they offered him gifts of gold, frankincense, and myrrh.* ¹²*And having*

been warned in a dream not to return to Herod, they left for their own country by
another road.

Because of the widespread expectation among the Jewish people of a coming messianic ruler, King Herod saw the news of a newborn king as a threat to his own power, and conflict became inevitable. He had taken upon himself the illegitimate title "King of the Jews" as well as assumed the prerogative of a royal son of David by rebuilding the temple in Jerusalem. His ostentatious living, opulent building projects, excessive taxation, and murderous cruelty laid a heavy burden on the peasant population. As Rome's point man in Judea, he was insanely distrustful of any perceived threats to his power. His apparent interest in the child was deceitful, for he intended to destroy Jesus, not pay homage to him.

The wise men from the East, avid scholars of spiritual mysteries, undertook an arduous journey to honor the child of whom great things were prophesied. Whether these seekers were from Persia, Arabia, Babylon, or other places to the East, their significance is that they were Gentiles from distant nations. Later tradition embellished the biblical account by giving names and royal titles to these magi: Melchior, king of Persia; Gaspar, king of India; and Balthasar, king of Arabia. The wise men interpreted the rising of the star as a heavenly sign marking the birth of a great ruler. In the days of Moses, a seer from the East named Balaam had blessed Israel's future by proclaiming a coming king who would be announced by a star: "A star shall come out of Jacob, and a scepter shall rise out of Israel" (Num 24:17). The text of the gospel states that the star was not just any unusual cosmic occurrence, but "his star," a divine sign pointing to the Messiah.

The scene sets up a strong contrast between the paranoid fear of King Herod and the adoring homage of the wise men. It is the first public acknowledgement of the identity of Mary's child, but it also reveals a looming peril. While Herod plots the death of the child, the strangers from the East anticipate all the believers from all the nations who will be called to salvation through the new king from the line of David. For this Son of David is also Son of Abraham, in whom all the nations of the earth are destined to be blessed. The origins of Jesus point to his destiny. During his public ministry, some accepted him and did him homage; others rejected him and sought to put him to death. From his birth, Jesus is destined to be the suffering Messiah whose worldwide dominion will bring salvation to all the nations.

Throughout the account of Jesus' infancy in Matthew's gospel, Joseph is much more prominent than Mary. Matthew traces Jesus' genealogy through Joseph. The angel appears to Joseph three times. It is Joseph who leads the Holy Family to Bethlehem. However, at the scene of the wise men coming to honor the newborn king, Mary takes center stage: "On entering the house, they saw the child with Mary his mother; and they knelt down and paid him homage" (verse 11). They offer him gifts worthy of a king. Surprisingly, Joseph is not mentioned at all in this section. This close link between royal child and his mother in such a regal context brings to mind Israel's queen-mother tradition. If Jesus is indeed the newborn king of the Jews, then Mary, as the mother of the king, is understood as the queen mother. The homage paid to the king, born in Bethlehem of Judah, the city of David, evokes the distinctive importance of the *Gebirah*, the "Great Lady," of the newborn or newly installed king in the dynasty of King David. "The child with Mary his mother" brings to mind the way the books of Kings repeatedly introduced each new Davidic king alongside the queen mother.

Reflection and discussion

- What can I learn about God from those outside my own religion?

- Why would the coming of the Messiah evoke such a violent response from some and such a welcome from others?

- What are the indicators in this scene that point to Mary as the queen mother of the newborn king?

- In what ways does this scene anticipate the acknowledgment of Mary as queen and mother of all nations?

Prayer

King of all the nations, you mark my path with your shining light and guide me on my journey to you. Help me open my heart to you and your royal mother and present to you the gifts of my own life.

**Then Joseph got up, took the child and his mother by night,
and went to Egypt, and remained there until the death of Herod.**
MATTHEW 2:14–15

Joseph Takes the Child and His Mother to Egypt

MATTHEW 2:13–18 ¹³*Now after they had left, an angel of the Lord appeared to Joseph in a dream and said, "Get up, take the child and his mother, and flee to Egypt, and remain there until I tell you; for Herod is about to search for the child, to destroy him." ¹⁴Then Joseph got up, took the child and his mother by night, and went to Egypt, ¹⁵and remained there until the death of Herod. This was to fulfill what had been spoken by the Lord through the prophet, "Out of Egypt I have called my son."*

¹⁶When Herod saw that he had been tricked by the wise men, he was infuriated, and he sent and killed all the children in and around Bethlehem who were two years old or under, according to the time that he had learned from the wise men. ¹⁷Then was fulfilled what had been spoken through the prophet Jeremiah:

¹⁸"A voice was heard in Ramah,
*   wailing and loud lamentation,*
Rachel weeping for her children;
*   she refused to be consoled, because they are no more."*

Although the dreams of Joseph carry the narrative forward, confirming that God is orchestrating events and protecting the Messiah, the center of attention is the child Jesus and his mother, Mary. In each episode,

Matthew repeats the phrase "the child and his mother" (verses 11, 13, 14, 20, 21). This focus on the messianic child along with his mother reflects the central role of the king's mother in the birth, enthronement, and reign of the kings in David's line. The queen mother was enthroned with the king and enjoyed a position of great honor during the reign of her son and often kept her position even after her son's death. Alluding to this prominent tradition, Matthew's narrative emphasizes the role of the mother of the Messiah in the kingdom inaugurated by Jesus Christ.

While the star of the newborn king shines forth, there are those who seek to blot out that light. In his raging fury, Herod attempts to eliminate his newborn rival. When the wise men refuse to tell Herod the location of the child, he ordered the murder of "all the children in and around Bethlehem who were two years old or under" (verse 16). The text evokes images of terrifying escape, deadly swords and blood-red pavement, frantic parents desperately trying to save their children, and wails of inconsolable grief. The young family, escaping in the night to Egypt, exiled in a foreign land, carries memories of horror and regret for those who did not escape. The text accurately depicts the character of Herod, who indulged in well-attested acts of cruel brutality. He had three of his own children put to death, and to ensure proper mourning at his own funeral, he instructed his soldiers to kill notable political prisoners at the news of his death so that all Judea would weep for him.

The holy family stands in agonized solidarity with the millions of refugees throughout history and down to the present, uprooted from their homes, separated from family members, wracked with fear and anxiety, struggling to survive in a harsh world. Joseph would have lived as a foreign worker, willing to do even the most menial tasks to survive. Their exile reflects the political situation of first-century Jews under Roman rule. Using military terror to intimidate their subjects, the imperial occupiers created countless refugees, desperate to protect their families and survive. The narrative is all too relatable for Matthew's readers in his own time and today.

The evangelist continues to shape the narrative by inserting fulfillment citations from the Old Testament, showing that the life of Jesus recapitulates the history of Israel. Recall that the family of Jacob went down to Egypt to seek refuge from famine, how Moses was rescued from the evil intent of Pharaoh to kill the male babies, and how the Hebrew slaves were liberated from their enslavement in Egypt. "Out of Egypt I have called my son" (verse 15) quotes the words of Hosea, referring now to Jesus but harking back to the original exodus of God's children. The context of the passage from the prophet offers a tender, parental view of God for those who wait in hope: "When Israel was a child I loved him, and out of Egypt I called my son....I took them up in my arms....I was to them like those who lift infants to their cheeks. I bent down to them and fed them" (Hos 11:1–4). This God who loves his people affectionately is the Father of Jesus, who cares for him in his infancy. The coming of the Messiah offers new hope for God's people, a hope rooted in the exodus and proclaimed by the prophets, that God will again redeem his people and lift them out of darkness.

The next citation from the prophets recalls the weeping of Rachel as the children of Israel are led into exile (verses 17–18). The words of Jeremiah refer now to the mothers of Bethlehem but harken back to the deportation of the captive people of God centuries before (Jer 31:15). With these two citations, Matthew echoes the two most definitive events in Israel's history, the exodus and the exile, connecting the endangered Messiah with the saving narrative of his people.

The vulnerable child is never alone but is always in the company of his mother, surrounded by her instinctively fierce care, which exposes her to the same perils. Harsh military and political power govern the narrative, but at its heart is "the child and his mother," vulnerable, courageous, compassionate. The child's close brush with death will become all too real in a few decades. His mother's fears will take a sharp, personal turn when the powers of the imperial state will kill her son too. Already the shadow of the cross falls over the Christmas crib. While Rachel still weeps for her children everywhere, we can trust that divine light will overcome the darkness.

Reflection and discussion

- Why does Matthew focus my attention on "the child and his mother" in each episode?

- What is the gospel teaching me about Jesus and Mary by associating them with the exodus and exile of their ancestors in Israel?

- In what ways do my parental instincts remind me of God's love?

Prayer

God of Israel and Father of Jesus, you have shown your constant and faithful love in every age. Help me to place my home in your steady care and know that your love for me will not leave me abandoned.

> "Get up, take the child and his mother, and go to the land of Israel,
> for those who were seeking the child's life are dead."
>
> MATTHEW 2:20

Joseph Brings the Child and His Mother from Exile

MATTHEW 2:19–23 ¹⁹*When Herod died, an angel of the Lord suddenly appeared in a dream to Joseph in Egypt and said,* ²⁰*"Get up, take the child and his mother, and go to the land of Israel, for those who were seeking the child's life are dead."* ²¹*Then Joseph got up, took the child and his mother, and went to the land of Israel.* ²²*But when he heard that Archelaus was ruling over Judea in place of his father Herod, he was afraid to go there. And after being warned in a dream, he went away to the district of Galilee.* ²³*There he made his home in a town called Nazareth, so that what had been spoken through the prophets might be fulfilled, "He will be called a Nazorean."*

Each of the four episodes in Matthew's second chapter is related to a place associated with a key feature of salvation history. Bethlehem harks back to God's choice of David (verses 1–12); Egypt recalls God's decision to free Israel from bondage (verses 13–15); Ramah is a reminder of Israel's captivity in Babylon (verses 16–18); Nazareth anticipates the life of Jesus (verses 19–23). Each episode also contains an Old Testament citation that includes the name of the place. In this way, Matthew demonstrates that the events surrounding the Messiah's advent happen in a way that "fulfilled" the Scriptures of Israel—that is, in accord with God's plan. The quoted passages serve as a key to help us understand the events of Christ's coming more deeply by recalling the larger context of each episode as part of the history of God's salvation.

In this final episode of Matthew's introductory narrative, Herod has died and Joseph is directed to take "the child and his mother" back to Israel (verse 20). But Joseph is again warned in a dream that the brutal Archelaus has inherited his father's rule in Judea. The reign of the new tyrant began with the massacre of thousands of people, and he was so despised by the people that he was eventually deposed by Rome. To avoid this cruelty, Joseph guided his family north to Galilee, where they settled in the town of Nazareth.

Although Matthew sees this move as one more way in which the Scriptures are fulfilled, there is actually no text in the Old Testament that contains the words "He will be called a Nazorean" (verse 23). Most probably Matthew sees a wordplay with the Hebrew word *netzer*, which means "branch," and alludes to the prophet Isaiah: "A shoot shall come out from the stock of Jesse, and a branch shall grow out of his roots" (Isa 11:1). Matthew shows that Jesus is that branch growing from the root of Jesse, the father of King David, again highlighting Jesus' identity as the messianic king from the line of David.

While these opening chapters of Matthew's gospel demonstrate that the coming of Jesus is in continuity with the exodus, the Davidic monarchy, the exile, and all that has come before him, it also shows how his coming is a completely new action of God. By looking back into ancient Israel and forward into the ministry of Jesus, these narratives show us how the new grows out of the old, and the old finds fuller expression in the new. Matthew's gospel continues to demonstrate that all the claims made for Jesus in his infancy will be realized throughout his saving life and that Jesus the Nazorean is indeed the messianic king of God's people.

Reflection and discussion

- What are the places where God has led me as part of his saving plan?

- How does God use prophecy, dreams, faith, and circumstances to guide Joseph and his family? Which does God use to guide my life?

- Why is it so essential for me as a Christian to know the Old Testament?

Prayer

Merciful Father, you guided the family of Joseph, Mary, and Jesus from place to place to protect them and to fulfill your will. Safeguard me and lead me to the places where I can best experience your presence and serve you.

**"Is not this the carpenter's son? Is not his mother called Mary?
And are not his brothers James and Joseph and Simon and Judas?
And are not all his sisters with us?"** MATTHEW 13:55–56

The Family of Mary in Nazareth

MATTHEW 13:54–58 [54]*He came to his home town and began to teach the people in their synagogue, so that they were astounded and said, "Where did this man get this wisdom and these deeds of power?* [55]*Is not this the carpenter's son? Is not his mother called Mary? And are not his brothers James and Joseph and Simon and Judas?* [56]*And are not all his sisters with us? Where then did this man get all this?"* [57]*And they took offense at him. But Jesus said to them, "Prophets are not without honor except in their own country and in their own house."* [58]*And he did not do many deeds of power there, because of their unbelief.*

When Jesus returned to his hometown of Nazareth following his initial ministry around the Sea of Galilee, he was not received well by the townspeople. Upon entering the synagogue to teach, many who were him were "astounded," yet their shock does not lead to faith but to a series of skeptical questions. Their questions are legitimate, but they seem to be raised with an accusing and judgmental spirit. They have heard reports about what Jesus has been doing, but they question the source of his wisdom and power. For all they knew, Jesus was simply the son of the village carpenter and the woman they knew as Mary. So, "they took offense at him," unable to imagine that his man from their own town could inaugurate the kingdom of God. Their preconceived ideas about how God would act and should act become an obstacle that hinders their belief. They cannot reconcile the ordinariness of the man they have known for years and the wisdom and deeds of power of the one who stands before them.

Among their queries, they asked about the "brothers" and "sisters" of Jesus: "And are not his brothers James and Joseph and Simon and Judas? And are not all his sisters with us?" (verses 55–56). Who are these four brothers and multiple sisters of Jesus? Some suppose that these are simply more children borne by Mary and Joseph after the birth of Jesus, based on Matthew's earlier statement: "[Joseph] had no marital relations with her until she had borne a son" (1:25). Yet not having sex "until" a child is born tells us nothing about marital relationships after. The use of the word "until" in other passages (1 Samuel 15:35; 2 Samuel 6:23; Matthew 12:20) demonstrates more clearly that the conjunction does not imply that they lived in a different condition afterward. Likewise, to say that Jesus was Mary's "firstborn" son does not suggest that she had other children after Jesus. The term "firstborn" designates a legal status in the Torah that simply indicates that no children were born to Mary before Jesus.

These brothers and sisters of Jesus are never described in the gospels as children of Mary. The ancient church held that Mary remained a virgin before, during, and after the birth of Jesus, and her perpetual virginity was virtually unquestioned until modernity. For this reason, interpreters suggest that these brothers and sisters of Jesus are not full siblings of Jesus, but perhaps step-siblings, cousins, or close relatives. One early position, based on the second-century apocryphal gospel, the *Protoevangelium of James*, holds that the brothers and sisters are the older children of Joseph. When Joseph is chosen by the high priest to be the husband of Mary, he protests, "I already have sons and am old." But Joseph agrees to the marriage and brings his children with him, making Jesus the youngest of at least seven children.

The most common position through the ages has held that these "brothers and sisters" are actually Jesus' cousins, children born either to Mary's sister or to Joseph's sister or brother. At the crucifixion scene, "Mary the mother of James and Joseph" is named as one of the women at the cross of Jesus (Matt 27:56). John's crucifixion scene describes this Mary as "his mother's sister, Mary the wife of Clopas" (John 19:25). This position produces the unlikely result of two sisters both named Mary. Instead, Clopas may be the brother or brother-in-law of Joseph, thereby making Mary the mother of Jesus the sister-in-law of Mary the mother of James and Joseph. Both Hebrew and Aramaic, lacking a specific word for "cousin," used "brother" to refer to a wide range of kinship relationships. The Greek terms *adelphos* (brother) and *adelphe* (sister) also admit a wider meaning than full siblings.

From all this related data, we know that James and Joseph were not Jesus' siblings, and thus the most plausible interpretation is that Simon, Jude, and the "sisters," along with James and Joseph, are all close cousins of Jesus. It is also probable that the other Mary, the mother of James and Joseph, is not the sibling of Mary but her sister-in-law, cousin, or other close relative.

There was little distinction in ancient cultures between the nuclear family and the extended family. Since the mortality rate was high, especially maternal mortality associated with childbirth, most families were, in fact, blended families. The repeated appearance of this extended family throughout the gospels indicates that they grew up together. Even if these cousins of Jesus did not all live under one roof, they formed part of his extended, blended family. Perhaps these relatives lived in adjoining houses and shared a courtyard. Whatever the case, Mary must have engaged in a lot of direct and indirect parenting of a large brood. Such parenting required all the energy and common sense required of good childrearing, and it produced an abundance of noise, messiness, conversation, and laughter. Sharing a courtyard dinner with nine or ten family members while discussing religion and politics must have contributed to the formation of Jesus as an effective speaker, teacher, and debater.

Reflection and discussion

- What is the meaning of the proverb quoted by Jesus: "Prophets are not without honor except in their own country and in their own house"? Is this saying also true today?

- What seems to me to be the best explanation of the relationship of the "brothers" and "sisters" to Jesus?

- How does imagining Jesus growing up in a large extended and blended family challenge my view of the holy family as father, mother, and single child?

- What factors have caused us to neglect the extended family and focus on the nuclear family today? What have we lost in doing so?

Prayer

Son of God and Son of Mary, your divine presence and power is manifested through your humanity. Challenge my rigid ideas about how God should act and help me be wise and humble enough to believe in you.

SUGGESTIONS FOR FACILITATORS, GROUP SESSION 3

1. Welcome group members and ask if anyone has any announcements to make.

2. You may want to pray this prayer as a group:
   God our help in ages past, who has constantly shown your faithful love, you bring new hope to your people through the pregnancy of women and the birth of children. Through the legacy of our spiritual ancestors, you have prepared the world for the coming of the Messiah. Help us to trust that your love will not leave us abandoned and give us confidence in the maternal help of your daughter Mary. May we be wise and humble enough to hope in your saving design and to be witnesses of your plan for the world.

3. Ask one or both of the following questions:
   - Which thought from the lessons this week stands out most memorably to you?
   - What is the most important lesson you learned through your study this week?

4. Discuss lessons 7 through 12. Choose one or more of the questions for reflection and discussion from each lesson to discuss as a group. You may want to ask group members which question was most challenging or helpful to them as you review each lesson.

5. Remember that there are no definitive answers for these discussion questions. The insights of group members will add to the understanding of all. None of these questions requires an expert.

6. After talking about each lesson, instruct group members to complete lessons 13 through 18 on their own during the six days before the next group meeting. They should write out their own answers to the questions as preparation for next week's group discussion.

7. Ask the group if anyone is having any particular problems with the Bible study during the week. You may want to share advice and encouragement within the group.

8. Conclude by praying aloud together the prayer at the end of one of the lessons discussed. You may add to the prayer based on the sharing that has occurred in the group.

> **"Do not be afraid, Mary, for you have found favor with God. And now, you will conceive in your womb and bear a son, and you will name him Jesus."** LUKE 1:30–31

Called to Give Birth to the Messiah

LUKE 1:26–33 ²⁶*In the sixth month the angel Gabriel was sent by God to a town in Galilee called Nazareth,* ²⁷*to a virgin engaged to a man whose name was Joseph, of the house of David. The virgin's name was Mary.* ²⁸*And he came to her and said, "Greetings, favored one! The Lord is with you."* ²⁹*But she was much perplexed by his words and pondered what sort of greeting this might be.* ³⁰*The angel said to her, "Do not be afraid, Mary, for you have found favor with God.* ³¹*And now, you will conceive in your womb and bear a son, and you will name him Jesus.* ³²*He will be great, and will be called the Son of the Most High, and the Lord God will give to him the throne of his ancestor David.* ³³*He will reign over the house of Jacob for ever, and of his kingdom there will be no end."*

Mary was powerless in a world in which power ruled, young in a society that valued age, poor in a culture divided into classes, and female in a world run by men. Yet, this scene of Gabriel's announcement to her in the small town of Nazareth expresses an astonishing reality. Despite her vulnerability, youth, poverty, and gender, God chooses her as the perfect instrument for bringing salvation into the world. She finds her status and identity in her obedience to God and participation in his divine plan.

The angelic birth announcement follows a pattern of such announcements throughout Scripture, linking Mary with the great sweep of God's gracious history with Israel. Yet, God's intervention in the life of Mary contains elements unlike anything that came before it. The insistence that Mary is a "virgin" highlights the radical newness of God's action (verse 27), even though she is also "engaged" (betrothed) to Joseph. The Jewish betrothal is the first stage of the marriage process; their consent has been exchanged in the presence of witnesses, but they have not yet begun to live together. Mary is still living in her family home and not yet under the same roof as her husband. So, why does Luke mention that Mary is a virgin, especially since most betrothed women would be virgins, and why would he state it twice in the same verse? He is preparing for the rest of the angel's announcement of the unique, virginal conception of the Messiah.

The first words spoken to Mary are these: "Greetings, favored one! The Lord is with you" (verse 28). Although this simple greeting doesn't seem very significant at first glance, we must examine it further to understand why Mary was "much perplexed" by it and why she "pondered what sort of greeting this might be" (verse 29).

The initial greeting may also be translated "Rejoice" (*Chaire*, in Greek) and is meant to bring to mind the prophetic summons for the people of Israel to be glad: "Sing aloud, O daughter Zion; shout, O Israel! Rejoice and exult with all your heart, O daughter Jerusalem!" (Zeph 3:14). What is the reason for such rejoicing? "The Lord is with you"—that is, "The king of Israel, the Lord, is in your midst" (Zeph 3:15), so, "Do not be afraid, Mary" (Luke 1:30) and "Do not fear, O Zion" (Zeph 3:16). Mary represents Israel as faithful "daughter Zion" to whom Zephaniah announced the long-awaited advent of the Messiah. This coming of Israel's king is exactly what Gabriel announces is being fulfilled in Mary. She is told to rejoice because the Lord is coming in the most profound way—within her womb. She unites in her person the desires and hopes of all God's people.

Gabriel greets Mary as the "favored one," literally, "she who has been graced" (*kecharitomene*, in Greek). The traditional wording "full of grace" (*gratia plena*) comes from the Latin Vulgate of St. Jerome. The single Greek word is more of a title for Mary than a description of her, taking the place of her given name when she is addressed by the angel. Grammatically, the title is the perfect passive participle form of the verb in the feminine singular. This means that her being filled with grace is not something about to happen to her as a result of the angel's message but rather is an action completed in the past with effects that continue in the present. In view of the mission she is about to receive, Mary has already been transformed by divine grace and continues to be graced by God. The title tells us something important about who she is. No one in all of Scripture besides Mary is addressed with this exalted title. God has blessed her with this grace unlike any person before her as he has prepared her to become the mother of his Son.

Despite Mary's perplexity and her pondering, she does not allow her troubled feelings to turn her away from what the Lord is asking of her. The angel's next words, "Do not be afraid, Mary" (verse 30), repeat word's given to Mary's ancestors throughout the Old Testament, assuring them that God is present with them as they are called to some great mission in God's plan. God looks upon Mary with such favor that he is willing to entrust his own Son to her. Gabriel reveals that Mary will become a mother: "You will conceive in your womb and bear a son" (verse 31).

Luke presents Mary's vocation as mother of the Messiah within the framework of the kingdom of David. She is introduced in the narrative as being betrothed to a man who is "of the house of David" (verse 26). Luke mentions Joseph's royal heritage because it is his adoptive parentage that makes Jesus also a royal heir. The angel describes Jesus to his mother in ways that recall the covenant promises God gave to David about his everlasting dynasty. He will be called "the Son of the Most High" (verse 32), a title indicating his filial relationship with God. As God said to David, "Your house and your kingdom shall be made sure forever before me; your throne shall be established for ever" (2 Sam 7:16), Jesus will complete the promises given in God's covenant with David. Although the tribes of Israel were divided and the kingdom split in two and taken into exile, God's promises had not failed. The hopes of a future Messiah who would restore Israel were fulfilled in Jesus. God will give to him David's throne: "He will reign over the house of Jacob for ever, and of his kingdom there will be no end" (verse 33). With these words, Gabriel is clearly identifying the child of Mary as the long-awaited Messiah and giving Mary the honored vocation of being the queen mother. By speaking these words directly to Mary, the angel evokes her royal maternity and all the implications of Mary's queenship.

Reflection and discussion

- In what ways is the identity of Mary dependent on the identity of her son Jesus?

- Why would God prepare Mary with divine grace in anticipation of the conception of her divine Son?

- How does the Annunciation convey the truth that Jesus is Israel's Messiah and that Mary is the queen mother?

Prayer

Most High God, you surprised and blessed Mary with the revelation of your plan for her life. Show me how to work with your grace in trust and humility, responding to you like Mary, your grace-filled daughter.

Then Mary said, "Here am I, the servant of the Lord; let it be with me according to your word." LUKE 1:38

Mary's Response to the Word of God

LUKE 1:34–38 ³⁴*Mary said to the angel, "How can this be, since I am a virgin?"* ³⁵*The angel said to her, "The Holy Spirit will come upon you, and the power of the Most High will overshadow you; therefore the child to be born will be holy; he will be called Son of God. ³⁶And now, your relative Elizabeth in her old age has also conceived a son; and this is the sixth month for her who was said to be barren. ³⁷For nothing will be impossible with God." ³⁸Then Mary said, "Here am I, the servant of the Lord; let it be with me according to your word." Then the angel departed from her.*

The question Mary asks of the angel is quite puzzling: "How can this be, since I am a virgin?" (verse 34). Why would a betrothed woman be bewildered after being told that sometime in the future she will conceive a child? After all, this is the usual course when couples reach the second stage of marriage and start engaging in marital relations. The angel's announcement so far has not indicated Mary's immediate conception but seems to point to the conception and birth of a child in her future married life. If Mary was planning on consummating her marriage with Joseph in the near future, there would be no reason to ask, "How can this be?"

Mary's question to the angel, then, suggests that she has no intention to consummate her marriage. She raises the question because she has made a decision to remain a virgin throughout her life. This view is common throughout Christian history and was advanced by Saints Gregory of Nyssa, Augustine,

66

Thomas Aquinas, Bonaventure, and many more. Dedicating oneself to God through virginity was not a widespread ideal within Judaism, yet it was not completely unknown in the world in which Mary lived. It seems that Jeremiah, John the Baptist, Jesus, Paul, and some Jewish Essenes also remained celibate.

Because lifelong virginity was not as socially feasible in the first century as it is today, Mary's marriage to Joseph would have provided her with economic stability and social protection. According to Numbers, which establishes regulations for vows made by women, the key for determining whether the vows of a married woman are binding is the consent of her husband (Num 30:6–8). Joseph must have agreed with Mary's dedication to virginity and of course would have remained celibate himself throughout their marriage. In retrospect, God led Mary to marriage while she remained a virgin to protect her reputation in the future, when she would conceive her child by the Holy Spirit. The same divine guidance that inspired Mary to choose virginity also guided her marriage to Joseph so that the child to be born would be raised in a family setting suited to healthy growth and stability.

Following Mary's perplexed query, the angel gives her the most remarkable part of his announcement: Mary will conceive this child not through natural means but as a virgin through the power of the Holy Spirit (verse 35). The Holy Spirit that will come upon Mary recalls the divine spirit/breath/wind (*ruah* in Hebrew) at the creation of the cosmos and of human beings (Gen 1:2; Job 33:4; Jdt 16:14). This creative Spirit of God will bring about the new creation, which is the incarnation of Christ in the womb of Mary. This new creation also anticipates the Spirit of God coming upon the disciples at Pentecost. As Luke begins his gospel with this descent of the Holy Spirit upon Mary to conceive the Messiah, he begins the Acts of the Apostles with the descent of the same Spirit upon the disciples to conceive the church.

In a parallel phrase, the angel declares that "the power of the Most High will overshadow" Mary (verse 35). This image recalls the cloud of God's glory that overshadowed the tabernacle at Mount Sinai (Exod 40:34–35). Luke uses this same image at the scene of the transfiguration, where he describes the divine glory present in the cloud overshadowing the disciples (Luke 9:34). With this image, Luke is inviting his readers to understand Mary as God's new tabernacle, the new vessel of God's presence among his people.

Gabriel has thus revealed to Mary the twofold identity of her soon-to-be-born child. He will be the Messiah, the one given the throne of King David with an everlasting kingdom, and he will be the Son of God, because he will be conceived through the overshadowing power of the Holy Spirit. The church's earliest theology, reflected in Paul's writings, expresses this dual nature of Mary's child: "descended from David according to the flesh" and "Son of God with power according to the spirit" (Rom 1:3–4). This divine king will come not in terrible glory, blinding light, or trumpet blast. He will come through Mary's womb, a hungry and crying child, the hope of all the world.

As a sign to confirm the announcement to Mary, the angel reveals the pregnancy of Elizabeth, her elderly and previously barren kinswoman (verse 36). Elizabeth is able to conceive a child for the same reason Mary will conceive as a virgin: "Nothing will be impossible with God" (verse 37). The Old Testament contains instances of barren women unexpectedly becoming pregnant, including Israel's matriarch Sarah. But never in history has a virgin conceived a child. So how will Mary respond to this invitation? She gets the last word in the dialogue with Gabriel and her response is exemplary: "Here am I, the servant of the Lord; let it be with me according to your word" (verse 38). Mary receives the word of God in her heart and thus consents to conceive the Son of God in her womb. As a woman of God's word and the first to hear the gospel proclaimed, she becomes in Luke's gospel the first and ideal disciple.

Reflection and discussion

- How might Mary have felt about the angel's message? How can her acceptance give me courage and hope?

- What aspects of Mary's dialogue with the angel suggests that she had already chosen a life of virginity?

- In what areas of my life do I need to hear the words of the angel: "Nothing will be impossible with God"?

- What would I like to imitate in Mary's response to God's will: "Here am I, the servant of the Lord; let it be with me according to your word"?

Prayer

Lord God, as I continue to study the life of Mary in the gospels, you desire to bring good news to my life too. Help me to look for unexpected messages and to anticipate the new ways you wish to work in my life.

Elizabeth was filled with the Holy Spirit and exclaimed with a loud cry, "Blessed are you among women, and blessed is the fruit of your womb."
LUKE 1:41–42

Elizabeth Praises the Mother of the Lord

LUKE 1:39–45 *39In those days Mary set out and went with haste to a Judean town in the hill country, 40where she entered the house of Zechariah and greeted Elizabeth. 41When Elizabeth heard Mary's greeting, the child leaped in her womb. And Elizabeth was filled with the Holy Spirit 42and exclaimed with a loud cry, "Blessed are you among women, and blessed is the fruit of your womb. 43And why has this happened to me, that the mother of my Lord comes to me? 44For as soon as I heard the sound of your greeting, the child in my womb leaped for joy. 45And blessed is she who believed that there would be a fulfillment of what was spoken to her by the Lord."*

Informed by the angel of Elizabeth's remarkable pregnancy, Mary set out for a journey of several days to the hill country of Judea to visit her kinswoman. We can assume that Mary traveled this distance to assist her elderly relative with her upcoming birth, but the young, pregnant Mary also needed the counsel and encouragement of this wise older women in her own difficult situation. Mary did not turn to the men in her life—not to Joseph her husband for understanding, nor to her father for protection, nor to the priests for blessing. She travels to receive the kind of consolation that can come only from another woman.

During pregnancy, mothers-to-be wait for the stirring of new life within them. It is a time of expectant longing and anticipation, the emotions that the church seeks to stir within itself, especially during the season of Advent. In this scene we witness the private sphere of two pregnant women supporting one another and reflecting on how God is acting in their lives. Mary has traveled with haste to greet her relative; Elizabeth feels the leaping of the child in her womb and receives a revelation from the Holy Spirit of what God has done for Mary.

The two women represent the meeting of the old covenant and the new covenant. Elizabeth is elderly and will have a son who will be the last great figure of ancient Israel. Mary is young and will have a son who will usher in the new age of salvation. In Mary, the new covenant reaches out to the old, affirming its crucial significance in God's plan and preparing for its culmination. In Elizabeth, the old covenant recognizes its own fulfillment and honors the coming of the new. The joyful unity of these two women expresses the harmony between the traditional faith of Israel and the coming of the Savior, a completion and a new beginning of God's saving work in the world.

Elizabeth's twofold declaration of God's blessing praises Mary both in her own right and for the child she bears in her womb (verse 42). First, she proclaims of Mary, "Blessed are you among women." God has exalted Mary among all the women of the ancient covenant—Sarah, Rachel, Hannah, Deborah, Jael (Judg 5:24), and Judith (Jdt 13:18)—for Mary has been chosen to bring forth the one awaited by all past generations. These women of Israel were instruments of God's saving will, either by bringing forth new hope through their children or by delivering God's people from their enemies. Second, Elizabeth's exclamation "and blessed is the fruit of your womb" echoes the promise God made in the Torah to those who listened and obeyed the word of the Lord (Deut 28:4).

Elizabeth is overwhelmed that her young relative would come to her home, and she calls Mary by an exalted title: "mother of my Lord" (verse 43). In the Old Testament, "Lord" (*kyrios* in Greek) is both a royal and divine title: the designation of the king from the line of David and the Greek translation of God's personal name. Here it is used for the first of many times in Luke's writings for the royal and divine Messiah. Mary is thus the royal mother of the divine king, the one given the later Christian title *Theotokos*, the God-bearer, she who gave birth to God on earth. In acclaiming Mary as the Lord's mother, Elizabeth acknowledged first that Jesus was the Lord from the beginning of his earthly existence in Mary's womb, and second that Mary remains the mother of the Lord always because she conceived and gave flesh to the one who will reign forever, human and divine, in heaven.

The words of Elizabeth end with a final declaration of praise of Mary: "Blessed is she who believed that there would be a fulfillment of what was spoken to her by the Lord" (verse 45). Thus, Mary is praised both as mother of the Lord and as a model for Christian believers. Mary is the ideal disciple because she is committed to God's word. She is a hearer and a doer of the word. After receiving the good news of Christ, she hastens to share that word. She surrenders herself to God's plan, she is full of gratitude for the gifts she receives, and she has a contemplative sense of wonder at the mysteries of God. She is truly a woman of the word.

Reflection and discussion

- What aspects of the joyful faith of Elizabeth and Mary would I like to imitate?

- What parts of this narrative remind me that Mary is the ark of the new covenant, the fulfillment of the sacred, golden ark brought by David to Jerusalem (2 Sam 6)?

- How could my life be enriched if I shared the intimacy of faith with a trusted relative, friend, or spiritual guide?

Prayer

Holy One of Israel, you have raised up women of courage and faith among all the generations of your people. Help me to wait in hope, like Elizabeth and Mary, for the fulfillment of your saving promises.

"My soul magnifies the Lord, and my spirit rejoices in God my Savior,
for he has looked with favor on the lowliness of his servant."

LUKE 1:46–48

Mary Rejoices in God's Merciful Salvation

LUKE 1:46–56

⁴⁶And Mary said,
"My soul magnifies the Lord,
   ⁴⁷and my spirit rejoices in God my Savior,
⁴⁸for he has looked with favor on the lowliness of his servant.
   Surely, from now on all generations will call me blessed;
⁴⁹for the Mighty One has done great things for me,
   and holy is his name.
⁵⁰His mercy is for those who fear him
   from generation to generation.
⁵¹He has shown strength with his arm;
   he has scattered the proud in the thoughts of their hearts.
⁵²He has brought down the powerful from their thrones,
   and lifted up the lowly;
⁵³he has filled the hungry with good things,
   and sent the rich away empty.
⁵⁴He has helped his servant Israel,
   in remembrance of his mercy,

^{55}*according to the promise he made to our ancestors,*
    to Abraham and to his descendants forever."
^{56}*And Mary remained with her about three months and then returned to*
her home.

After Mary and Elizabeth share their fears, grapple with God's intentions for their lives, find courage, and express their hopes, they are able to move forward with more confidence and joy despite the challenges they face. Now Mary, swelling with new life by the power of the Spirit, sings out with her whole being—her soul and her spirit—with body, mind, and strength. This canticle of Mary, chanted by the one Elizabeth addressed as "mother of my Lord," is one of the most beautiful songs of Scripture.

Since Mary knew the Old Testament well, she would have been quite familiar with the passages from the Scriptures of Israel that echo throughout her song of praise. She uses titles for God she would have known from her scriptural prayer—Lord, Savior, and Mighty One—and she knows that God's name is holy (verses 46–49). She is part of a long line of biblical women who chant poetic canticles: Miriam (Exod 15:20–21), Deborah (Judg 5), Hannah (1 Sam 2:1–10), and Judith (Jdt 16:1–17). Mary's song particularly resonates with the Psalms, the daily hymns of the Jewish people. She sings back to God the truths that she learned in her daily reflection on the word of God.

The song demonstrates that Mary is the representative of God's people. The mercy shown to her reflects the mercy that God has shown to Israel and is a response to the promises God made long ago. The young Mary yields herself completely to God's will and sings with complete confidence that what had been promised has now come to pass. She is a model of living faith because she recognized what God was doing through her, she accepted it joyfully, and she was humble enough to give God all the glory.

The song speaks of Mary's humility: she was mindful of her status as a simple village maiden whose "lowliness" the Lord has regarded with favor (verse 48). God has unexpectedly reversed her low status so that now she can sing, "all generations will call me blessed." Likewise, God reverses all that people have come to expect: he disperses the arrogant, throws down the rulers, and sends the rich away empty. But God also lifts up the lowly, fills the hungry, and comes to the aid of Israel (verses 51–54). What God has done for Mary models and anticipates what God will do for the poor, oppressed, and powerless of the world.

It is striking that the lines that speak of what God promised through the prophets for the future age to come is proclaimed in the past tense. In this way, the song expresses confidence and certainty in God's establishment of justice and mercy. Mary is so sure that God will do what is promised that she proclaims it as an accomplished reality. In Mary's song of the God who raises the lowly and brings down the mighty, who fills the hungry while sending the rich away empty, Luke is introducing a theme prominent throughout his writings. This reversal expected for the time of judgment has already begun, and God's choice of Mary is evidence of it.

Mary prayed this canticle not for herself alone but for all of us, to pray these words after her. When we do so, we are placed in an intense relationship with the living God, our overflowing source of joy and hope, who looks upon the struggling people of the world with deep compassion and summons us to engage together in what God does, to turn the unjust order of things upside down and make the world right again.

Reflection and discussion

- What are some similarities between Mary's song and the songs sung by Miriam, Deborah, Hannah, and Judith?

- How does Mary teach me the importance of studying the Scriptures of ancient Israel?

- How does Mary's song describe the qualities of the coming reign of Christ?

- What seem to be some of the emotions Mary felt as she chanted this canticle of praise?

Prayer

God my Savior, you have looked upon me with favor and you continually reverse my expectations. Show me your power, your holiness, and your mercy, which you have shown in every age.

She gave birth to her firstborn son and wrapped him in bands of cloth, and laid him in a manger, because there was no place for them in the inn. LUKE 2:7

Mary Gives Birth to Her Son

LUKE 2:1–7 ¹*In those days a decree went out from Emperor Augustus that all the world should be registered.* ²*This was the first registration and was taken while Quirinius was governor of Syria.* ³*All went to their own towns to be registered.* ⁴*Joseph also went from the town of Nazareth in Galilee to Judea, to the city of David called Bethlehem, because he was descended from the house and family of David.* ⁵*He went to be registered with Mary, to whom he was engaged and who was expecting a child.* ⁶*While they were there, the time came for her to deliver her child.* ⁷*And she gave birth to her firstborn son and wrapped him in bands of cloth, and laid him in a manger, because there was no place for them in the inn.*

Mary and Joseph travel from the small village of Nazareth and enter a drama initiated by a decree from the heart of the Roman Empire so that "all the world" is on the move (verse 1). Luke's narrative doesn't say how the couple reached Bethlehem from Nazareth, but traveling on foot was the usual means of travel for the poor. On donkey or on foot, the journey would have been exhausting. Mary's belly is a globe as round and full as the earth. The life inside her is about to become the life for the world.

When the time comes for Mary's delivery, the couple lacks adequate security and housing. Giving birth in the first century would have been like childbirth in some war-ravaged area of our world today. Emperors and their armies oppressed the people; corruption and extortion were a way of life. With "no place for them in the inn" (verse 7), it seems that they take shelter in a cave where animals are stabled. Despite the romantic glow of many Christmas scenes, the conditions were probably rather dreadful, more like giving birth in some abandoned hovel of an urban alleyway today.

In this unfamiliar, uncomfortable situation, Mary gives birth. She wraps her child in bands of cloth, the traditional way of securing a newborn. The swaddling clothes provide warmth and restrict the movement of the limbs, helping the infant to sleep. Mary then laid him in a manger, a feeding trough for domesticated animals. It could have been a movable wooden feeding box or, more probably, a stone trough or a low depression on a rocky ledge of the cave. While it served the purpose of cradling a baby, its previous use removed any pretense about the ease of this nativity scene. These two details, wrapped in bands of cloth and laid in a manger, will be the sign given to the shepherds by the angels. They may also be a sign anticipating Jesus' death, when his body will be "wrapped" in a cloth and "laid" in a rock-hewn tomb (Luke 23:53).

The description of Jesus as Mary's "firstborn son" (verse 7) is not intended to refer to the size of Mary's family and does not indicate that Mary must have had other children. Rather, the term designates that Jesus holds the legal status associated with the firstborn. According to the Torah, the firstborn would be consecrated to God (Exod 13:2; Num 3:13) and receive the father's inheritance (Deut 21:17).

This firstborn of Mary is also proclaimed in the New Testament as the firstborn of God, just as Israel and the king of David's line were proclaimed God's firstborn in the Old Testament. Jesus is the "firstborn of all creation" (Col 1:15) and God's firstborn in the world (Heb 1:6). The spiritual children of Mary in the future will be those who follow Jesus, since he is the "firstborn within a large family" (Rom 8:29).

Traditional Christian teaching holds that Mary gave birth as a virgin, without the pains of labor, since pain in giving birth was a punishment due to sin (Gen 3:16). As the mother of the Messiah, Mary was preserved free from sin in order to be the perfect vessel of the incarnation. The liturgical and artistic tradition of the church has held that Christ was born at night, and more specifically at midnight. The birth of light came into a world of darkness. As Isaiah says, "The people who walked in darkness have seen a great light" (Isa 9:2). The birth of Christ "when half-spent was the night" is a long-held belief rooted in the poetic words of the Wisdom of Solomon: "While gentle silence enveloped all things, and night in its swift course was now half gone, your all-powerful word leaped from heaven, from the royal throne, into the midst of the land that was doomed" (Wis 18:14–15). And the fact that the earliest icons of Christ's birth depict him surrounded by reverent animals comes from a reading of Isaiah: "The ox knows its owner, and the donkey its master's crib; but Israel does not know, my people do not understand" (Isa 1:3). The church's theological, liturgical, and artistic tradition is rich with expressions of the meaning and significance of the Messiah's birth from the virgin Mary.

Yet, we also know that the nativity of Christ was physical and genuine. As the divine child shivered in the cold, Mary tenderly clasped him to her heart and with great joy warmed him against her breast. Then she handed the child to Joseph, who pressed him to his chest and thanked God for this moment. Together they gave praise and cherished the holy night when Christ was born.

Reflection and discussion

- What are some indications that the shadow of the cross falls over the Christmas crib?

- What are some of the lessons Luke wants to teach me through the circumstances of Jesus' birth?

- What are some of the Old Testament allusions that have become the source of our Christmas traditions?

- Which liturgical and artistic expressions of Christmas do I most cherish?

Prayer

Lord of heaven and earth, in the blackness of the half-spent night, you sent the world's light to shine in our darkness. Awaken me to come and adore the newborn child, wrapped in swaddling clothes and lying in a manger.

"Do not be afraid; for see—I am bringing you good news
of great joy for all the people: to you is born this day in the city
of David a Savior, who is the Messiah, the Lord."

LUKE 2:10–11

The Shepherds
Find Mary, Joseph,
and the Child

LUKE 2:8–20 *⁸In that region there were shepherds living in the fields, keeping watch over their flock by night. ⁹Then an angel of the Lord stood before them, and the glory of the Lord shone around them, and they were terrified. ¹⁰But the angel said to them, "Do not be afraid; for see—I am bringing you good news of great joy for all the people: ¹¹to you is born this day in the city of David a Savior, who is the Messiah, the Lord. ¹²This will be a sign for you: you will find a child wrapped in bands of cloth and lying in a manger." ¹³And suddenly there was with the angel a multitude of the heavenly host, praising God and saying, ¹⁴"Glory to God in the highest heaven, and on earth peace among those whom he favors!" ¹⁵When the angels had left them and gone into heaven, the shepherds said to one another, "Let us go now to Bethlehem and see this thing that has taken place, which the Lord has made known to us." ¹⁶So they went with haste and found Mary and Joseph, and the child lying in the manger. ¹⁷When they saw this, they made known what had been told them about this child; ¹⁸and all who heard it were amazed at what the shepherds told them. ¹⁹But Mary treasured all these words and pondered them in her heart. ²⁰The shepherds returned, glorifying and praising God for all they had heard and seen, as it had been told them.*

The thrilling and consoling news of the Messiah's birth is announced by the heavenly angel to the shepherds, "keeping watch over their flock by night," and the divine glory shone around them. They were filled with intense fear by the appearance, but the messenger calmed them, "Do not be afraid; for see—I am bringing you good news of great joy for all the people" (verses 8–10). Of all the human race, those who merited to be the first to see the Christ Child were the lowliest laborers of the land, the humble shepherds of Bethlehem.

The angel's message proclaimed the birth of "a Savior, who is the Messiah, the Lord" (verse 11). These three titles of Jesus—Savior, Messiah, and Lord—describe his mission as it develops throughout Luke's writings. "Savior" points to his role as the one who delivers God's people. "Messiah" designates his regal office as the promised Anointed One of God. "Lord" indicates his sovereign authority. Although Jesus is born under the reign of Caesar Augustus, these titles are as majestic as those of the emperor. For Luke, the key historical figure of the era is not the Roman emperor but the frail child Jesus, the royal Savior and Lord of all people.

Yet, throughout the life of the Messiah, from beginning to end, he was exposed and vulnerable, from the cave of his birth to the cave of his burial. We see beyond Mary's holding Jesus in her arms as a baby to Michelangelo's *Pietà* with Mary holding Jesus across her lap once more, his head resting on her shoulder. The "sign" is given to the shepherds: "You will find a child wrapped in bands of cloth and lying in a manger" (verse 12). The bands of cloth that wrapped his infant body become the linen cloth that wrapped his body for burial. The one who was laid in a manger would be laid in a rock-hewn tomb.

A host of angels then sing a two-part hymn of praise: "Glory" is offered to God in heaven and "peace" is given to people on earth (verses 13–14). Three word pairs show the relationship between the two parts: glory and peace, heaven and earth, God and "those whom he favors." First, God is glorified for who he is and what he has done. The heavens rejoice and praise God for the manifestation of salvation, the unfolding of redemptive history culminating in the birth of Jesus. Second, peace is extended to those upon whom God had extended his grace. The people who welcome the coming of Jesus Christ are the focus of heaven and earth.

The shepherds then make the short journey from their fields to the town of Bethlehem to see the event that God had made known to them. Perhaps they gathered some suitable gifts for the family: a young goat, a basket of eggs, and a bunch of dates. Arriving toward dawn, they found the grotto-stable and saw the child in the manger. They made known what the angels revealed to them during the night, to the amazement of all who heard.

As the shepherds depart giving praise to God with joyful hearts, we are left with the scene of Mary, who "treasured all these words and pondered them in her heart" (verse 19). The fullness of the significance of her Son is not immediately apparent, so she keeps on mulling over the words concerning the identity of Jesus. To "treasure" means to preserve, remember, and cherish. To "ponder" means to puzzle out their meaning, to toss them together until they make more sense. As Mary experiences these things that she doesn't fully understand, she engages in deep reflection. She turns them over in her mind, weighing them, letting them sink in, seeking to work out their meaning. She tries to put together her many thoughts into an understandable whole in order to grasp the depth of what God is showing her. This meditative pondering of God's word is the invitation that Luke offers to all his readers through Mary, the woman of the word.

Reflection and discussion

- Why does God first reveal the birth of Christ to shepherds?

- In what ways does a spirit of joy permeate the narrative of Christ's birth in the face of its obvious hardships?

- How did the titles of Jesus announced by the angel to the shepherds become politically subversive in the Roman Empire?

- What does Mary teach me about meditation and contemplation, showing me how to treasure and ponder the word of God?

Prayer

God in the highest heaven, bring joy and peace to your people on earth. Help me to treasure and ponder your word so that I may understand your will and be an instrument of your salvation for others.

SUGGESTIONS FOR FACILITATORS, GROUP SESSION 4

1. Welcome group members and ask if anyone has any questions, announcements, or requests.

2. You may want to pray this prayer as a group:
   Lord of heaven and earth, who sent the world's light to shine in our darkness, you brought good news to the world through the message of an angel. Show us your power, your holiness, and your mercy, which you have shown in every age. Teach us how to work with your grace in trust and humility and to respond to you like Mary, your grace-filled daughter. As we continue to study the life of Mary in the gospels, help us look for unexpected messages and anticipate the new ways you wish to work in our lives.

3. Ask one or both of the following questions:
   - What is the most difficult part of this study for you?
   - What insights stand out to you from the lessons this week?

4. Discuss lessons 13 through 18. Choose one or more of the questions for reflection and discussion from each lesson to discuss as a group. You may want to ask group members which question was most challenging or helpful to them as you review each lesson.

5. Keep the discussion moving but allow time for the questions that provoke the most discussion. Encourage the group members to use "I" language in their responses.

6. After talking over each lesson, instruct group members to complete lessons 19 through 24 on their own during the six days before the next group meeting. They should write out their own answers to the questions as preparation for next week's session.

7. Ask the group what encouragement they need for the coming week. Ask the members to pray for the needs of one another during the week.

8. Conclude by praying aloud together the prayer at the end of one of the lessons discussed. You may choose to conclude the prayer by asking members to pray aloud any requests they may have.

They offered a sacrifice according to what is stated in the law of the Lord, "a pair of turtle-doves or two young pigeons."
LUKE 2:24

Mary and Joseph Fulfill the Precepts of the Torah

LUKE 2:21–24 *²¹After eight days had passed, it was time to circumcise the child; and he was called Jesus, the name given by the angel before he was conceived in the womb.*
²²When the time came for their purification according to the law of Moses, they brought him up to Jerusalem to present him to the Lord ²³(as it is written in the law of the Lord, "Every firstborn male shall be designated as holy to the Lord"), ²⁴and they offered a sacrifice according to what is stated in the law of the Lord, "a pair of turtle-doves or two young pigeons."

The infancy of Jesus, though part of a universal drama, takes place within the world of Judaism. Luke observes that Mary and Joseph, following the birth of their son, did everything required by the Torah, "the law" of Israel. He refers specifically to three separate regulations: the circumcision and naming of the child (Gen 17:10–14), the purification of the mother forty days after the birth of a child (Lev 12:1–8) and the dedication of the firstborn son to God (Exod 13:2, 12–16).

Jerusalem and its temple are important for Luke's gospel to show readers how the life of Jesus and his church are rooted in ancient Israel, its worship, and its institutions. For this reason, the gospel begins and ends in Jerusalem, the symbolic center of Israel's faith, the focal point of Israel's memories and hopes. The Torah and the temple, ancient expressions of the covenant, form the context for God's new revelation. Mary and Joseph are shown as observant parents committed to the heritage of their ancestors.

Emphasizing Mary's partnership with Joseph, Luke writes, "they" brought the child up to Jerusalem; "they" offered the sacrifice (verses 22, 24). Throughout this episode, "the child's father and mother" act together for their son (verse 33). The two were bonded in marriage, adjusting to the care of a new infant, and seeking God's blessings together. Although Scripture and tradition emphasize the royal and virgin mother, it is also essential to honor her marriage to Joseph, the man with whom she shared her life, for better or for worse.

Eight days after his birth, they circumcise Jesus, cutting the covenant into his very flesh in the tradition of Abraham. They name him Jesus, the name given by Gabriel at the angel's announcement to Mary. Forty days after his birth, they go up to Jerusalem to carry out the ritual of purification and to present their child to God. Arriving at the temple, the family climbs the great staircase and enters Solomon's Portico. There they purchase a pair of doves for the offering. Again, the family is portrayed as among the poor of the land. According to the Torah, when the days of her purification are complete, a woman shall bring to the priest "a lamb in its first year" and a dove; but "if she cannot afford a sheep, she shall take two turtle-doves or two pigeons, one for a burnt-offering and the other for a sin-offering" (Lev 12:6–8). The offering itself expresses the family's status among the lower ranks of society.

At the Court of Women, Mary joins the column of mothers in Israel celebrating their childbirth in accord with the prescribed rituals. She presents her simple offering to the priest who kills the birds and presents them at the flaming altar of sacrifice. Unable to afford a lamb, Mary's offering foreshadows the end of the gospel, when Jesus will offer himself on the cross in sacrifice, "like a lamb that is led to the slaughter" (Isa 53:7).

The third ritual for the family to perform is the presentation of the first-born son to the Lord. According to the law given at Mount Sinai, every first-born male shall be consecrated to the Lord, set apart for sacrificial service to God (verse 22–23; Exod 13:2). But, because of Israel's sin of idolatry, this consecration was taken from the firstborn and given only to the faithful tribe of Levi. Afterward, every firstborn son from other tribes was required to be "redeemed," or bought back, at the "redemption price" of five shekels of silver, to be released from this service (Num 18:15-16). So, as a firstborn son from a non-Levitical tribe, it was expected that the parents of Jesus would redeem him from consecrated service to God.

What is exceptional about this scene is its lack of any description of redeeming Jesus, no mention of the five-shekel price. Instead, Mary and Joseph "present him to the Lord" (verse 22), handing him over to God in the temple. The language here is sacrificial, in that Jesus is given as an offering to the Father, the first act of his young life to prefigure his complete sacrifice on the cross.

Reflection and discussion

- Why does Luke emphasize that Mary and Joseph are faithful observers of the law of the Lord?

- Why is it so important to follow the legal prescriptions and ritual practices of my faith tradition?

- What do the instructions of my Christian faith require of me in order to consecrate and teach the next generation?

Prayer

Daughter of Israel, you followed the law of God and were committed to the heritage of your ancestors. Teach me to joyfully observe the teachings of your Son and help me to live as a member of the new covenant.

Simeon blessed them and said to his mother Mary,
"This child is destined for the falling and the rising of many
in Israel, and to be a sign that will be opposed." LUKE 2:34

A Sword Will Pierce Mary's Soul

LUKE 2:25–38 *²⁵Now there was a man in Jerusalem whose name was Simeon; this man was righteous and devout, looking forward to the consolation of Israel, and the Holy Spirit rested on him. ²⁶It had been revealed to him by the Holy Spirit that he would not see death before he had seen the Lord's Messiah. ²⁷Guided by the Spirit, Simeon came into the temple; and when the parents brought in the child Jesus, to do for him what was customary under the law, ²⁸Simeon took him in his arms and praised God, saying,*

²⁹"Master, now you are dismissing your servant in peace,
   according to your word;
³⁰for my eyes have seen your salvation,
     ³¹which you have prepared in the presence of all peoples,
³²a light for revelation to the Gentiles
     and for glory to your people Israel."

³³And the child's father and mother were amazed at what was being said about him. ³⁴Then Simeon blessed them and said to his mother Mary, "This child is destined for the falling and the rising of many in Israel, and to be a sign that will be opposed ³⁵so that the inner thoughts of many will be revealed—and a sword will pierce your own soul too."

³⁶There was also a prophet, Anna the daughter of Phanuel, of the tribe of Asher. She was of a great age, having lived with her husband seven years after her marriage, ³⁷then as a widow to the age of eighty-four. She never left the temple but worshiped there with fasting and prayer night and day. ³⁸At that moment she came, and began to praise God and to speak about the child to all who were looking for the redemption of Jerusalem.

T he presence of Jesus, Mary, and Joseph in the temple of Jerusalem, faithfully performing the ritual statutes of the Torah, sets the stage for their encounter with the elderly Simeon and Anna. Here are two representatives of Israel at its best. They are devout and righteous, at home in God's temple, moved by God's Spirit, longing for the fulfillment of God's promises, and awaiting the coming of God's salvation. They stand at the junction of the old covenant and the new, demonstrating that the hope revealed in Jesus is built on memory and that God's new work is the fulfillment of the promises of old.

Simeon has been promised by the Holy Spirit that he will see the Messiah before his death (verse 26). Now, taking the six-week-old Jesus in his arms, this devout old man praises God for keeping his word. He represents ancient Israel awaiting its Messiah with patience and expectancy. The old Israel can now rest peacefully as the new age of God's salvation begins. Simeon's song, like Mary's canticle, weaves his personal experience of God with what God is doing for all his people (verses 29–32). As God's salvation, Jesus is light both for the Gentiles and for Israel. Simeon's words preview the saving drama that will continue throughout Luke's gospel and his Acts of the Apostles, as Jesus is shown to be glory for the people of Israel and revelation to the Gentiles. He is the light of salvation to everyone on earth.

After this joyful song, Simeon speaks directly to Mary and prophesies that God's salvation will not be accomplished without great cost. Within Israel's sanctuary of ritual sacrifice, he portends the mysterious nature of Jesus' sacrificial life, which will provoke opposition and bring suffering to the life of Mary and her Son (verse 34). Anyone who brings light also creates shadows. The "sign" given to the shepherds will lead to the sign of Jesus crucified and buried. He will be a sign that will provoke a divided response within Israel, a sign that some will accept and others will reject.

Then, almost in a whisper, Simeon tells Mary that she will also pay a price for her intimate association with Jesus: "And a sword will pierce your own soul too" (verse 35). Mary will share deeply in the pain and rejection Jesus will experience. She who was the first to receive the good news will also experience within her own heart the full joy and grief of his saving life. As the ancient writers have said: "With great love comes great pain."

Our Lady of Sorrows teaches us that grace is almost always accompanied by grief. A life pierced with affliction is a tragedy from one point of view, but the wounds of suffering can enlarge the human heart. As mother and disciple, Mary can teach us how to unite the sufferings of our lives with the cross of Christ, how to suffer in ways that enlarge our hearts and help others see meaning and hope in the midst of pain.

Along with Simeon, the family encounters the prophet Anna. Remaining a widow after the early death of her husband, Anna chose a lifetime of service to God over remarriage. She is at the temple daily, fasting and offering prayers. Like Simeon, Anna points to Jesus and praises God for him. She addresses the crowd at the temple concerning the redemption of God's people. She testifies that God's decisive salvation has come in the child of Mary and Joseph. For those who await the consummation of God's saving plan, fulfillment has come.

Reflection and discussion

- How might Mary have felt when Simeon addressed the prophecy of the piercing sword to her? What does she teach me about suffering and sorrow?

- What virtues do I see in Simeon and Anna? How could I put one of their qualities into practice in my own relationship with God?

Prayer

Lord and Master, you ask me to wait with patience and hope as your will is gradually unfolded. Give me a deep longing for your presence and help me to trust that you are always faithful to the word of your promises.

The child grew and became strong, filled with wisdom; and the favor of God was upon him. LUKE 2:40

The Village Life of Nazareth

LUKE 2:39–40 *³⁹When they had finished everything required by the law of the Lord, they returned to Galilee, to their own town of Nazareth. ⁴⁰The child grew and became strong, filled with wisdom; and the favor of God was upon him.*

I n the ancient world, important people were supposed to come from important places. But the expected ways are rarely God's ways. Jesus, Mary, and Joseph made their home in a very out-of-the-way place in circumstances that were anything but privileged. No one wanted to move to Nazareth from Jerusalem, Caesarea, Tiberius, or any of the large cities of the land. This small village in lower Galilee was off the beaten path. It was not on any of the major Roman roads, and it was quite a distance from the commercially viable fishing villages around the Sea of Galilee. The town had a population of a few hundred at the most, and the young people yearned to leave for the larger cities with more abundant opportunities.

By all outward appearances, the life of the holy family could not have been more ordinary. Their home was built around a natural cave which served as part of the living space. These domestic caves were the only heating and cooling systems available, staying warm and dry in winter and pleasantly cool in summer. The one entrance to the home featured a hewn threshold and a wooden door. A few windows sat high in the walls, designed more for ventilation and lighting rather than scenic views. The rooms were used for preparing food, eating meals, sleeping, and storing the necessities of life. In one corner of the living room sat the frame and loom that Mary used for spinning and weaving threads into cloth. Pegs, hooks, and niches around the walls provided off-the-floor storage. The house included a room for Joseph's workshop, where he could work on rainy days and store his tools.

Excavations in Nazareth indicate that its inhabitants took advantage of the soft limestone to dig basements, cisterns, and storage bins underneath the ground level of their homes. Storage areas in the family home would have contained supplies of grain and milled flour for cooking, feed for animals, and chaff for plastering and brickmaking. Storage baskets near the kitchen held cheeses, dried fruits, and produce, and jugs held supplies of olive oil and wine. Clay lamps fueled with olive oil lit the dark rooms. The family ate meals while sitting cross-legged on the floor at a low table. The healthy Mediterranean diet, so touted today, was the daily fare: grains, olives, and grapes. Meals were served in clay pots, casserole dishes, and bowls. They often consisted of a stew with lentils and seasoned vegetables, ladled on pita bread, sometimes with cheese, yogurt, nuts, and fruit on the side. A cup of local wine took the edge off a hard day's work.

The family shared their home with the animals, especially the goats, which were family pets and sources for dairy products. People lived close to one another; the modern need for "personal space" was unheard of. The roof of the house also served as an important space for domestic activity. The family accessed the flat area by climbing an inside ladder or the outside stairs. They would often go to the roof to pray, visit with guests, dry their clothes, or take an afternoon siesta.

Much of the day-to-day life of Nazareth took place outdoors because the weather was generally mild throughout the year. The courtyard was shared by several families who lived in the adjoining houses. A fence wrapped a portion of the area for animal pens, and chickens roamed freely. The oven, made of clay bricks, sat in a corner of the courtyard, and the aroma of baking bread and cooking spices filled the air throughout the day. Women drew water from the one spring of the village and carried it to their homes in clay jars balanced on their heads.

An abundance of olive trees, which grew easily on the rocky hillsides, surrounded the village. The communal olive press extracted the olive oil, so essential for lamp fuel, cooking, and ointments. Vines with deep purple grapes spread out over the slopes of the hill. The villagers harvested the grapes and trampled the fruit in the grape presses to make syrup, vinegar, and wine. Various grains, including barley, wheat, and millet, grew in the fields around Nazareth. They cultivated fig and pomegranate trees as well as gardens with legumes and vegetables. The residents of this out-of-the-way hamlet worked toward one goal: self-sufficiency. If they could grow all they needed, pay their taxes, and not make trouble for the Roman authorities, they could live a pleasant life.

Usually, one's hometown has at least one claim to fame—but not Nazareth. Neither the Jewish Scriptures nor any of the ancient Jewish historians made a single reference to Nazareth. People from the cities knew little about the town; it was the kind of place that city folk ridiculed. The derogatory comment made by Nathaniel, "Can anything good come out of Nazareth?" (John 1:46), typified the response of outsiders.

Yet, Nazareth did have one special quality. The town was set on a mountainous ridge, about 1,650 feet above sea level at its highest point. An afternoon stroll to the south of the town would offer a panoramic view of the Jezreel Valley below. Few places are more significant for the long history of Israel than this vast plain below hilly Nazareth. The stretch of the valley formed part of the ancient Via Maris, the Way of the Sea, connecting Egypt in the southwest with Damascus in the northeast. For centuries, caravans of traders and mighty armies had passed through this valley. Mary and Joseph must have come here often with their son to watch the travelers pass far below. Perhaps they imagined that their child would eventually leave Nazareth and have an opportunity to make an impact in the larger world.

There is no way this family could imagine the global impact their simple life would have. Seldom are we able to understand the full significance of our daily words and actions. But the "branch" grown from the root of Jesse and David did indeed blossom and bear fruit for the world. For two millennia, the people of the world have journeyed to the small village of Nazareth for inspiration because the Son of Mary called this place home.

Reflection and discussion

- What is significant about the fact that the life of the holy family was outwardly insignificant and ordinary in every way?

- What most strikes me about the home of Mary in Nazareth?

- How might the gaze of Jesus into the Jezreel Valley have influenced his developing understanding of his messianic mission?

Prayer

Blessed are you, Lord our God, who has sanctified us with your commandments and brings forth food from the earth. Bless our home and our family, our meals and our work, and keep us in your holy presence all the days of our life.

He went down with them and came to Nazareth, and was obedient
to them. His mother treasured all these things in her heart.

LUKE 2:51

The Astonished
Parents of Jesus

LUKE 2:41–52 ⁴¹*Now every year his parents went to Jerusalem for the festival of the Passover.* ⁴²*And when he was twelve years old, they went up as usual for the festival.* ⁴³*When the festival was ended and they started to return, the boy Jesus stayed behind in Jerusalem, but his parents did not know it.* ⁴⁴*Assuming that he was in the group of travelers, they went a day's journey. Then they started to look for him among their relatives and friends.* ⁴⁵*When they did not find him, they returned to Jerusalem to search for him.* ⁴⁶*After three days they found him in the temple, sitting among the teachers, listening to them and asking them questions.* ⁴⁷*And all who heard him were amazed at his understanding and his answers.* ⁴⁸*When his parents saw him they were astonished; and his mother said to him, "Child, why have you treated us like this? Look, your father and I have been searching for you in great anxiety."* ⁴⁹*He said to them, "Why were you searching for me? Did you not know that I must be in my Father's house?"* ⁵⁰*But they did not understand what he said to them.* ⁵¹*Then he went down with them and came to Nazareth, and was obedient to them. His mother treasured all these things in her heart.*

⁵²*And Jesus increased in wisdom and in years, and in divine and human favor.*

The family was the bearer of Israel's religious tradition, so all the earliest education of Jesus in the faith occurred in his home. Mary and Joseph nurtured a strong awareness of the presence of God in their home not only through their words but also through their activities: lighting the Sabbath lamps, making the foods and symbols of Israel's feasts, and offering sung prayers of praise and thanksgiving. Both at home and in the synagogue, Jesus learned the ancient Hebrew language of his people and studied the sacred traditions of Israel. He read the Torah and the prophets and chanted the psalms, so that by his early adolescence, he was ready to become a full member of the people of Israel.

Jesus must have traveled often with his family to Jerusalem for the pilgrimage feasts of Israel. The journey was long, requiring several days on the road. Since travel was dangerous, families would always make the journey with their extended families, or they would join a caravan with hired guards. Adults and children alike eagerly awaited the feasts. Jews from countries throughout the Roman world would flock to Jerusalem. They came from Syria, Asia Minor, Babylon, Greece, Egypt, and Rome. Along the trails winding through the land resounded the songs of the festive travelers. In Jerusalem during the festival days, people could feel the pulse of the entire Jewish people. They would meet in the street every type of Jew from every corner of the world and see how they lived. Jerusalem was the home of all Jews, and people like Mary and Joseph felt more at home in Jerusalem than anywhere else on earth.

On the afternoon before Passover, Joseph would purchase a choice lamb from the market and bring it to the temple to be ritually slaughtered in sacrifice. He would then take it to the inn or home where they were staying, roast it, and eat it with his extended family in a group of ten or more. They mixed strong wine with water and drank it from ceremonial cups, and they ate bitter herbs and other traditional foods of the Passover with newly baked unleavened bread.

All children like to ask questions, and clever parents do things that provoke the kinds of questions that enhance their children's religious education. One of these questions has been ritualized in the Passover meal as the youngest child at the table asks, "Why is this night different from all other nights?" Then begins the narrative recounting God's deliverance from the slavery of Egypt. The questions of children become teaching opportunities for parents to explain the traditions of their people and to instill a reverence for God within their hearts.

Wherever in the world Jews celebrate Passover, the moon is always full on that night. The meal concludes with a final blessing and singing. Following the sacrificial meal, the family strolls back outside, where the bright moon cast a silvery gleam over the flat roofs of the city. Again the streets of Jerusalem are filled with promenading Jews, natives and pilgrims side by side. The family moves from one group to another, greeting friends and making new ones. By this time, the priest has reopened the gates of the temple precincts, where Jesus, Mary, and Joseph spend the rest of the night along with thousands of other pilgrims, praying and singing hymns of praise to God.

At the conclusion of the festival, the family joins the caravan of Nazarenes for the long trip back home. After a day's journey, as they settle down for the night, Mary and Joseph search for their adolescent son, assuming he has been in the caravan with his cousins and friends. When they are unable to find him, they fear he is lost among the pilgrims back in Jerusalem. They frantically return and search the city, finding him in the temple, talking with the teachers of Israel, who are amazed at his wisdom (verses 46–47). Mary is astonished, angry, and bewildered: "Child, why have you treated us like this? Look, your father and I have been searching for you in great anxiety" (verse 48). Jesus replies in a way his parents could not understand: "Why were you searching for me? Did you not know that I must be in my Father's house?" (verse 49).

"My Father's house" refers to the temple and all associated with God's dwelling on earth. This is the first time in the gospels that Jesus calls God his Father. *Abba*, the affectionate term that Jesus used for Joseph, he now uses to designate his eternal Father. Mary and Joseph begin to realize that their son's life will not be focused on the carpentry trade, that perhaps their son is destined for something much bigger than Nazareth can offer. Their home in Nazareth will no longer be the center of their son's world; rather, the house of God and all the concerns of his Father God will consume his mind and heart. But Jesus returns to Nazareth and remains obedient to them (verse 51). Like any Jewish child of the time, Jesus honors his father and mother, responds to their instructions, and respects their parental authority throughout his life. The home of Mary and Joseph and the "Father's house" will not compete for the attention of Jesus. He honors both houses by living as Son of Mary and Son of God.

Reflection and discussion

- Why is faith taught to children not only through words but through activities and rituals?

- What do I do when children seem "lost"—wandering from their faith, rebelling as adolescents, estranged from the family?

- The third-century theologian Origen said, "Learn from Mary to seek Jesus." How is Mary teaching me to seek Jesus?

Prayer

Father God, you chose Mary as the mother of your Son so that she could teach me to seek Jesus. Help me to trust as she trusts, to search as she searches, and to treasure his words in my heart as she does.

> But he said to them, "My mother and my brothers are
> those who hear the word of God and do it."
> LUKE 8:21

The Mother and Family of Jesus

LUKE 8:19–21 ¹⁹*Then his mother and his brothers came to him, but they could not reach him because of the crowd.* ²⁰*And he was told, "Your mother and your brothers are standing outside, wanting to see you."* ²¹*But he said to them, "My mother and my brothers are those who hear the word of God and do it."*

11:27–28 ²⁷*While he was saying this, a woman in the crowd raised her voice and said to him, "Blessed is the womb that bore you and the breasts that nursed you!"* ²⁸*But he said, "Blessed rather are those who hear the word of God and obey it!"*

Luke's readers are given an invitation throughout the gospel to be among the ones who hear, believe, and obey the word of God. These will form the true family of Jesus. Having walked with Jesus and listened to Jesus' teachings by reading the gospel, we are left with a choice. Will I be a member of his family?

This scene of the mother and brothers of Jesus follows immediately after two parables of Jesus. In the first, the word of God is described as scattered seed. Although the seed always has the potential to germinate, only that sown on good soil will take root, grow up, and bear fruit. In the second parable, the word of God is depicted as the fire of a lamp. It can only be effective in lighting up a room when it is not hidden, when it is placed on a lampstand. Both parables are about the ineffectiveness or the effectiveness of the word of God. How we receive the word of God is crucial. "Pay attention to how you listen," Jesus says, indicating that he wants his disciples to listen to his teaching, reflect on it in their heart, and respond to it by putting it into practice.

The scene in which the family of Jesus, "his mother and his brothers" (verse 19) come to see him and are unable to reach him because of the size of the crowd reinforces the teaching of Jesus concerning the word of God. The family of Jesus, he says, consists of "those who hear the word of God and do it" (verse 21). This is not a repudiation of Jesus' natural family because Mary herself is shown throughout Luke's writing to be the ideal disciple. But in the priorities of Jesus, the bonds of faith are superior to the ties of blood. His brothers and sisters are those who nurture the seed of God's word, allowing it to bear fruit in the world, and those who allow his word to shine brightly like a lamp to those around them.

The second scene builds upon the first as a woman in the crowd around Jesus cries out, "Blessed is the womb that bore you and the breasts that nursed you!" (verse 27). Since a mother in Jewish society is honored through the accomplishments of her son, the praise of Mary is also an expression of gratitude to Jesus. The cry from the crowd echoes the cry of Elizabeth, "Blessed are you among women, and blessed is the fruit of your womb" (Luke 1:42), and fulfills Mary's prophecy, "From now on all generations will call me blessed" (Luke 1:48).

In response to the woman's declaration, Jesus offers a beatitude of his own, emphasizing the blessedness of "those who hear the word of God and obey it!" (verse 28). The saying summarizes a central teaching of Jesus expressed throughout Luke's gospel: blessings come to those who both listen to God's word and act on it (6:47; 8:15; 8:21). Although Mary is preeminent among those who listen and respond to God's word, all persons of all times and places are blessed when they hear and obey the word of God.

Reflection and discussion

- What obstacles prevent me from hearing, believing, and doing the word of God?

- Why does Jesus shift the emphasis from the womb and breasts of his mother to hearing and obeying the word of God?

- How can the family of disciples in my church or group become more like a family of parents and children in relationship to one another?

Prayer

Lord God, you form your people by instilling your word within them. Help me to embrace the Scriptures with a generous heart so that I may hear, believe, and do your word, making it effective for those around me.

All these were constantly devoting themselves to prayer, together with certain women, including Mary the mother of Jesus, as well as his brothers. ACTS 1:14

All Were Filled with the Holy Spirit

ACTS 1:12–14; *¹²Then they returned to Jerusalem from the mount called Olivet, which is near Jerusalem, a sabbath day's journey away. ¹³When they had entered the city, they went to the room upstairs where they were staying, Peter, and John, and James, and Andrew, Philip and Thomas, Bartholomew and Matthew, James son of Alphaeus, and Simon the Zealot, and Judas son of James. ¹⁴All these were constantly devoting themselves to prayer, together with certain women, including Mary the mother of Jesus, as well as his brothers.*

2:1–4 *¹When the day of Pentecost had come, they were all together in one place. ²And suddenly from heaven there came a sound like the rush of a violent wind, and it filled the entire house where they were sitting. ³Divided tongues, as of fire, appeared among them, and a tongue rested on each of them. ⁴All of them were filled with the Holy Spirit and began to speak in other languages, as the Spirit gave them ability.*

As Luke moves to his second volume, the Acts of the Apostles, he forms a transition from the life of Jesus to a new stage of salvation history: the age of the church. Luke began his gospel with the coming of the Holy Spirit upon Mary to give birth to Israel's Savior; Acts begins with the coming of the Holy Spirit upon Mary and the disciples to give birth to the church. As with Jesus, who was filled with the Holy Spirit throughout his saving mission to

Israel, the church will be filled with the Holy Spirit for its expanding mission to the world. Throughout Luke's inspired writings, Mary is a model for the kind of expectant faith in God's promises which Jesus desires for his church: "Blessed is she who believed that there would be a fulfillment of what was spoken to her by the Lord" (Luke 1:45).

Following the ascension of Jesus into heaven, the disciples travel the short distance over the steep descent from Mount Olivet and the equally steep ascent back into the city of Jerusalem and arrive at "the room upstairs" (verses 12–13). The eleven apostles are joined with "Mary the mother of Jesus," some of the women who had followed Jesus from Galilee, and some of Jesus' extended family (verse 14). This becomes the nucleus of the church that will be empowered for mission by the Father's gift of the Spirit. These nine days between the ascension and Pentecost are a significant pause between God's mighty acts, a novena in which the church's task is to wait and pray, "Come, Holy Spirit." The community must await God's grace with expectant hearts, seeking God's Spirit in fervent prayer.

The "certain women" who formed the early community of believers in Jerusalem were presumably those women who supported the ministry of Jesus out of their resources in Galilee: Mary, called Magdalene, Joanna, Susanna, "and many others" (Luke 8:2–3). This group of women, who followed Jesus from Galilee, was with him at his crucifixion and "stood at a distance" (23:49). These same women followed his body to the tomb, "they saw the tomb and how his body was laid" (23:55), and then were the first witnesses that the tomb was empty (24:10). This community of women disciples establish a continuous, moving connection from Galilee to the cross, to the tomb and resurrection, and finally to the coming of the Holy Spirit as the church begins. These women from Galilee certainly include "Mary the mother of Jesus," who is named separately by Luke because of her unique significance in the early church as Mother of the Lord.

The wind and fire of Pentecost dramatically signals the church's beginnings (Acts 2:1–4). The church is the creation of the Holy Spirit, firing up the hearts and loosening the tongues of believers, moving the emerging community to speak and act. Through the grace and power of the Spirit, they must now witness to the Messiah, bearing him forward in history, on behalf of the kingdom of God. Although we can't know with certainty the activity of Mary within the early church in Jerusalem, her presence there allows for some imaginative con-jecture. She must have shared her experiences and wisdom with the other dis-ciples when they gathered for the Eucharist. Imagine her conversations with Mary Magdalene, the leading witness to the risen Christ, and with Joanna, who followed Jesus despite her wealth and social prestige. Consider what advice and strategies she offered for the incipient challenges the church faced. Ponder the mystical prayer of Mary as she entered her later years, still on fire with the Holy Spirit and filled with grace.

The historical life of Mary was a journey of faith: from her simple home in Nazareth to Jerusalem's upper room, the church's first house church. From youth to marriage to widowhood, she lived through the stages of life keeping faith with her compassionate God. From the birth of her child in a stall for ani-mals to his torturous death on a cross to hearing him proclaimed Savior and Lord, she trusted in the promises of her faithful God. Through years of anxiety and trust, danger and risk, suffering and joy, hard work and sabbath rest, ques-tioning and pondering, the prayerful mother of the Messiah became the wise mother of his church.

Reflection and discussion

- Why is waiting and praying just as important for the church as programs and activities?

- Why does Luke choose to parallel the role of Mary and the Holy Spirit both at the beginning of the gospel and the beginning of the church?

- In what ways is Mary a model and inspiration for the newly emerging church?

- Since the Holy Spirit still searches for hearts willing to be transformed by grace, what quality of Mary do I want to receive in my heart?

- Why is Mary the mother of Jesus also acknowledged as the mother of his church?

Prayer

Come Holy Spirit, teach me how to wait and pray. As you sent your wind and fire upon the receptive Virgin Mary, send your transforming graces into my heart to make me a witness to Jesus, the Messiah and Lord.

SUGGESTIONS FOR FACILITATORS, GROUP SESSION 5

1. Welcome group members and ask if anyone has any questions, announcements, or requests.

2. You may want to pray this prayer as a group:
   Creating and Redeeming God, through the Torah and prophets, you teach your people to wait with patience and hope as your will is gradually unfolded. As you chose Mary among all women to be the mother of your Son, give us the ability to trust as she trusts, to search as she searches, and to treasure your word in our hearts like her. May we embrace the Scriptures with a generous heart so that we may hear, believe, and do your word, making it effective for those around us.

3. Ask one or both of the following questions:
   - What most intrigued you from this week's study?
   - What makes you want to know and understand more of God's word?

4. Discuss lessons 19 through 24. Choose one or more of the questions for reflection and discussion from each lesson to talk over as a group.

5. Ask the group members to name one thing they have most appreciated about the way the group has worked during this Bible study. Ask group members to discuss any changes they might suggest in the way the group works in future studies.

6. Invite group members to complete lessons 25 through 30 on their own during the six days before the next meeting. They should write out their own answers to the questions as preparation for next week's session.

7. Ask group members to name ways that their study of Mary is changing their everyday lives.

8. Conclude by praying aloud together the prayer at the end of one of the lessons discussed. You may want to conclude the prayer by asking members to voice prayers of thanksgiving.

And the Word became flesh and lived among us, and we have seen his glory, the glory as of a father's only son, full of grace and truth.

JOHN 1:14

Children Born of the Will of God

JOHN 1:9–14 ⁹*The true light, which enlightens everyone, was coming into the world.* ¹⁰*He was in the world, and the world came into being through him; yet the world did not know him.* ¹¹*He came to what was his own, and his own people did not accept him.* ¹²*But to all who received him, who believed in his name, he gave power to become children of God,* ¹³*who were born, not of blood or of the will of the flesh or of the will of man, but of God.* ¹⁴*And the Word became flesh and lived among us, and we have seen his glory, the glory as of a father's only son, full of grace and truth.*

The prologue of John's gospel is just as much a Christmas story as the birth accounts of Matthew and Luke are. In fact, this text has been the liturgical gospel for Christmas day since the early centuries of the church. Here there is neither angel nor manger, neither virgin mother nor shepherds. In John's account, the story of Jesus begins long before Bethlehem, in the realm of God's timeless eternity. There, "the Word" (*Logos* in Greek) existed with God, and from there "the Word became flesh and lived among us" (verse 14). The coming of the Messiah is traced back not only through ancient Israel and God's prophetic promises but, according to John, back to "the beginning."

Before the ages, "the Word was with God, and the Word was God" (John 1:1). The Word, we might say, is God's self-expression. A human word is, in a sense, the extension of a person into his or her environment; the divine Word is God's reaching out, revealing the divine nature and sharing the divine life. The Word is distinct from God, but there is no separation between God and the Word. It is like the sun and its light-giving and warmth-giving rays. The rays are the manifestation of the sun, reaching out into the world, sharing its nature, and giving life to the world.

The first expression of God's word was creation itself. Throughout history, God spoke the divine word through the Torah and the prophets and wisdom. Finally, this divine communication culminated in the fullest and ultimate Word, Jesus Christ himself. The mission of Jesus, the Word, is to reveal to us the hidden nature of God, to manifest God's presence in a way that we can understand, showing us by his life that God is loving, generous, merciful, and forgiving. In the incarnate Word, God "lived among us." Literally, he pitched his tent, taking up residence among his people in a way far more intimate than when God dwelt in the tabernacle or temple of Jerusalem.

John's prologue refers to the Word as "the true light," the light of the world, the light which "enlightens everyone" (verse 9). This motif of light and darkness is prevalent throughout John's gospel, describing the presence of Jesus Christ in the midst of earth's shadows and the darkness of sin, ignorance, and death. The glory of God is displayed for all to see in him, the light that shines triumphantly in a darkened world.

Like the other biblical writers, John tells us that the coming of the Messiah into the world is something for which we must be prepared. At his historical coming, "the world did not know him" and "his own people did not accept him" (verses 10–11). But John intends his gospel to help us receive him and believe in him, because through that faith we are given "power to become children of God" (verse 12). This new birth into the family of God is not a birth of blood or of sexual desire or of human will; it is rather "of God" (verse 13). John's gospel is an invitation to be born anew and share in that new life.

The eternal Word was born into frail, corruptible humanity. The Word-made-flesh now dwelling among us did not come about through a seismic shift in the orientation of creation but through the flesh and blood of Mary. The Word became flesh and entered the heart and the womb of the virgin of Galilee, protected by a delicate ribcage tabernacle within an ever-so-destructible body. Through her sheer availability and free acceptance, she became the locus of the Word's silent enfleshment. Amid the history of universal salvation, Mary stands as our reminder of the scandalous particularity of God's personal entrance into our world. We cannot spiritualize or mythologize our uncomfortably historical faith. The Father could only conceive the Incarnation of his Son along with this woman, from whom his Son would take flesh. Just as in Eden there took place the first espousals of man and woman, so in Mary there took place the first espousals of God and humanity, eternity and time. In the marriage ceremony of divine love, Mary said, "I will," and the Word was conceived in her.

Today, we understand the significance of this divine enfleshment in Mary even more. We know that she is far greater than a receptacle for the divine "seed" to grow within her, a vessel for growing bones and muscles. Being a mother and giving flesh to a child includes the child's genetic makeup, human qualities, and potential. The child truly shares the body of the mother, and the mother shares the body of the child. The woman who conceived, formed a body, and gave birth to God on earth is the indispensable heart of the Incarnation. She cooperated fully, with her free will and her entire body, in her Creator's plan to lift humanity out of the mire and give us a share in God's eternal life.

Reflection and discussion

- How are my words the extension of myself, my self-expression to others? Why is it so important, then, to be a person of my word?

- In what way is the prologue to John's gospel a Christmas story even though Mary is not explicitly mentioned?

- Why is John so insistent on the incarnation (enfleshment) of God in Jesus Christ?

- Why is Mary indispensable for the incarnation of God in human flesh? Why does it seem essential that she be sinless and full of grace?

- How have I been born anew into the eternal life of God's family?

Prayer

Word of God, through your remarkable descent into our humanity, you have shared our human nature so that we might share your divine nature. Help me to share your grace and truth with the world.

Jesus said to her, "Woman, what concern is that to you and to me?
My hour has not yet come." His mother said to the servants,
"Do whatever he tells you." JOHN 2:4–5

Mary Initiates the Ministry of Jesus

JOHN 2:1–10 *¹On the third day there was a wedding in Cana of Galilee, and the mother of Jesus was there. ²Jesus and his disciples had also been invited to the wedding. ³When the wine gave out, the mother of Jesus said to him, "They have no wine." ⁴And Jesus said to her, "Woman, what concern is that to you and to me? My hour has not yet come." ⁵His mother said to the servants, "Do whatever he tells you." ⁶Now standing there were six stone water-jars for the Jewish rites of purification, each holding twenty or thirty gallons. ⁷Jesus said to them, "Fill the jars with water." And they filled them up to the brim. ⁸He said to them, "Now draw some out, and take it to the chief steward." So they took it. ⁹When the steward tasted the water that had become wine, and did not know where it came from (though the servants who had drawn the water knew), the steward called the bridegroom ¹⁰and said to him, "Everyone serves the good wine first, and then the inferior wine after the guests have become drunk. But you have kept the good wine until now."*

Having examined the portrayal of Mary in the gospels of Matthew and Luke, we have seen how understanding the role of the queen mother in the royal tradition of King David can help us better understand Mary in the kingdom of her divine Son. As the "Great Lady" (*Gebirah*, in Hebrew), Mary reigns as the royal mother and chief advisor to the Messiah. In that role she serves as the advocate, looking after the needs of God's people and interceding for them before the throne of her Son.

At this first scene of Jesus' saving ministry in John's gospel, the wedding in Cana, Mary expresses her attentiveness and concern for the needs of others. When she notices that "the wine gave out," her compassion for the family prompts her to bring the concern to Jesus (verse 3). The scene serves as a pattern for Mary's intercession in Christ's church. At the wedding, she mercifully comes to the aid of people in need and brings those needs within the circle of the messianic mission of her Son. Within the church, Mary notices the needs of her children, then she brings those needs to Christ.

At Cana, the mother of Jesus facilitates the work of Christ by instructing the servants, "Do whatever he tells you" (verse 5). She models the type of confident trust that is the necessary precondition for the work of her Son. In response, Jesus finds a way to meet the needs of the hour by performing an unobtrusive miracle. Only Jesus' mother, the chief steward, a few servants, and Jesus' disciples knew what happened. There is no indication that the other guests realized what Jesus had done. By acting discreetly, Jesus saves the family from any embarrassment and avoids stealing the spotlight from the wedding.

The scene illustrates well Mary's role as advocate for the people. In her unique position as the mother of the king, she confidently turns to her royal Son for help in a way that no one else could. And when she presents those needs to her Son, Jesus responds to his mother's intercession quite powerfully. Not only does Jesus fulfill Mary's request, providing the wine that is lacking, but he supplies it in an abundant way that goes well beyond anyone's expectations— at least twenty gallons' worth times six stone jars (verse 6). Mary is portrayed as a powerful advocate, bringing the needs of the family to her Son so that they receive from him what they need.

Notice that no one asks Mary to intercede. While everyone else was distracted with celebrating the occasion, Mary just noticed something very important. Spotting the empty containers for wine, she didn't want the couple to be embarrassed by not having enough to serve their guests. Mary's intercession is like that for all the people of Christ's reign. We often live frenzied lives and fail to notice our deepest needs. When we maintain a relationship with Mary our mother, she notices the details in our lives that we overlook. Mary tends to what we need in every moment, even when we don't ask her. If Mary, unasked, is so prompt to help those in need, how much more so will she be to help those who call upon her and ask for her help.

Like the empty jars, our hearts must also be empty in order for us to receive the graces God desires for us. Most people walked by the empty jugs without a second thought. But Mary sees what is hidden; she knows the secrets of our hearts. When we come to her empty, she turns to her Son on our behalf. And then he transforms our emptiness into the finest wine, saved for last.

The most mysterious words of this narrative are also the most wondrous. Jesus responds to Mary's request with the words "Woman, what concern is that to you and to me? My hour has not yet come," declining to get involved. Jesus intends to say that it is not yet time for his manifestation as the Messiah, the time of his saving ministry. Yet, through Mary's confident persistence, Jesus provides abundant wine for the wedding feast. The response of Jesus indicates that, had the request come from anyone else, he would not have complied with it. But because it came to him from his mother, he could not refuse it. No one but Mary could move Jesus to do what he had not yet intended to do. In her role as mother of the Messiah, Mary expedites the moment of grace for her children.

It is perfectly natural in the Christian tradition to ask other people to intercede for us. During the first centuries, the believers wrote the names of their martyred loved ones on the walls of the catacombs: "Felicitatas, pray for us." "Claudius, help us." But the advocacy of Mary is the most powerful of all. No one who flees to her protection, implores her help, or seeks her intercession is left unaided.

Reflection and discussion

• In what areas of my life do I feel dry, empty, thirsty, and without wine?

- King Solomon addressed the queen mother saying, "Make your request, my mother; for I will not refuse you" (1 Kings 2:20). What gives me confidence in the advocacy of Mary in her Son's reign?

- From the early centuries, Mary has been evoked as Advocate on the people of God. What does this gospel scene teach about the quality of Mary's advocacy?

- Is there something in my life that needs Mary's intercession? Ask her to expedite the hour of grace for you.

Prayer

Lord Jesus, in some areas of my life, I have no wine. I am empty, dry, and thirsty. Through the intercession of your blessed mother, fill the stone jar of my heart to overflowing with your life-giving water, then turn the water into the wine of your abundant love.

After this he went down to Capernaum with his mother, his brothers, and his disciples; and they remained there for a few days.
JOHN 2:12

Jesus Accompanied by His Mother to Capernaum

JOHN 2:11–12 *¹¹Jesus did this, the first of his signs, in Cana of Galilee, and revealed his glory; and his disciples believed in him.*

¹²After this he went down to Capernaum with his mother, his brothers, and his disciples; and they remained there for a few days.

John's gospel alone describes the primary works of Jesus' ministry as "signs," that is, acts that reveal the glory of God working through Jesus the Messiah. Mary the mother of Jesus makes an appearance only twice in John's gospel: strategically, at the beginning and the end of Jesus' ministry. Mary initiates the first of Jesus' "signs" at the wedding feast in Cana (verse 11), and she is featured at the death of Jesus (19:25–27), the completion of all the signs. By petitioning Jesus to provide new wine for the guests, she introduces a series of signs that the evangelist narrates throughout the gospel until the end at the cross.

As Mary was introducing the first sign of Jesus at Cana, telling Jesus, "they have no wine," Jesus responded, "My hour has not yet come." Each sign in the ministry of Jesus brings us closer to the "hour" when Jesus will be lifted up on the cross. The impending hour arrives in its fullness as Mary stands beneath the cross of Jesus. When Jesus sees "his mother and the disciple whom he loved," he gives each of them to the other as "mother" and "son." The evangelist says, "from that hour the disciple took her into his own home." Immediately after, Jesus says,

"I thirst," and is given sour wine to drink, after which he says, "It is finished" and bows his head in death.

The first appearance of "the mother of Jesus" at Cana and her final appearance at the cross form in John's gospel an *inclusio*, a frame or bookends. At the wedding feast, Mary initiates a series of signs to be accomplished throughout the gospel, and at the cross, she is given a mission in relationship to the beloved disciple in Christ's church. In this way, the presence of Mary forms a frame for the ministry of Christ, guiding readers to understand that Mary has a unique and ongoing role in the new covenant. John is inviting his readers to take in what he narrates in the intervening chapters from Mary's contemplative viewpoint.

The fact that Mary is featured at the beginning and end of Jesus' ministry suggests the importance of her role throughout the life of Jesus. Luke strives for the same effect when he spotlights Mary's role in the conception and birth of Jesus and highlights her presence among the apostles in the upper room as the church in enlivened by God's Spirit. Certainly, Mary is present either explicitly or implicitly at all the joyful, luminous, sorrowful, and glorious mysteries of the world's salvation. John indicates that Mary was near Jesus, not only in Cana and Jerusalem, but also in other places throughout his ministry. In his brief notice that Mary went with Jesus, his brothers, and his disciples "down to Capernaum" (verse 12), the evangelist hints at the many locations of the gospel. The fishing village of Capernaum, along the northern shore of the Sea of Galilee, is the heart of Jesus' public ministry. Surely, the presence of Mary wove in and out of the life of Jesus, from his first sign to his climactic cross.

Another way in which Mary is implicitly present throughout John's gospel arises from the spiritual relationship between the mother of Jesus and his beloved disciple established at the cross. When the gospel tells us that the disciple "took her into his own home," John caring for Mary as a son cares for his mother and Mary caring for John as a mother cares for her son, it is suggesting a lasting attachment. This beloved disciple is also the witness to the life of Jesus and source of the content of John's gospel. In fact, the early tradition tells us that Mary lived with John, first in Jerusalem and then in Ephesus, where the gospel was eventually written.

If Mary had not lived in the home of John, the gospel would probably be very different. What John wrote in his gospel arose from their discussion over decades together and bore the marks of their mother-son relationship of mutual care. They must have pondered together the things that Jesus said and did during his life, each contributing to the understanding of the other. Mary would bring to these recollections the unique perspective of a mother who had known her Son intimately throughout his life. The gospel not only contains the testimony of these two key witnesses to the saving life of Israel's Messiah but reflects their minds and hearts as well. The reflective contributions of Mary must have had an enormous influence on the way John presented the life of Jesus to others. Her personal insight as the bearer of God incarnate and her contemplative spirit would have deeply influenced John's understanding of the life and mission of Jesus.

Reflection and discussion

- What does John hope to accomplish in his gospel by placing the appearances of Mary at the beginning and end of Jesus' ministry?

- In what ways might Mary have influenced John and enhanced the formation of his gospel?

- What difference does it make for me to contemplate the mysteries of Christ's life through the mind and heart of Mary?

Prayer

Lord Jesus, your ministry was influenced by the compassion of your mother in Cana of Galilee, in Capernaum, and up to Jerusalem. Teach me to reflect on the holy mysteries of your saving life through the heart of Mary so that I may grow in love for you.

When a woman is in labor, she has pain, because her hour has come. But when her child is born, she no longer remembers the anguish because of the joy of having brought a human being into the world. JOHN 16:21

The Pain and Joy of a Woman's Labor

JOHN 16:16–22 *16"A little while, and you will no longer see me, and again a little while, and you will see me." 17Then some of his disciples said to one another, "What does he mean by saying to us, 'A little while, and you will no longer see me, and again a little while, and you will see me'; and 'Because I am going to the Father'?" 18They said, "What does he mean by this 'a little while'? We do not know what he is talking about." 19Jesus knew that they wanted to ask him, so he said to them, "Are you discussing among yourselves what I meant when I said, 'A little while, and you will no longer see me, and again a little while, and you will see me'? 20Very truly, I tell you, you will weep and mourn, but the world will rejoice; you will have pain, but your pain will turn into joy. 21When a woman is in labor, she has pain, because her hour has come. But when her child is born, she no longer remembers the anguish because of the joy of having brought a human being into the world. 22So you have pain now; but I will see you again, and your hearts will rejoice, and no one will take your joy from you.*

We can hear the voice of Mary in John's gospel as he devotes much attention to offering consolation to the disciples. In comparison to the other gospels, John softens the language used to describe the coming trials of the Christian community. While in the other gospels Jesus emphasizes the anguish his disciples will endure and their need for perseverance in suffering, in John's gospel Jesus speaks of the feelings of sorrow and joy, rooted in a relationship of trust. "A little while, and you will no longer see me, and again a little while, and you will see me" is Jesus' euphemistic way of speaking about the painful separation to come and the confident hope of unity to follow (verses 16–19).

And what model does Jesus propose for the disciples as they are about to go through their intense trial? A woman giving birth: "When a woman is in labor, she has pain, because her hour has come. But when her child is born, she no longer remembers the anguish because of the joy of having brought a human being into the world" (verse 21). Perhaps we hear an echo of Mary's maternal voice in these consoling words of Jesus.

Of course, both the harsh and soft language of the gospels are effective. Often, good parents use both on their children. One parent will tell the children to be strong, not holding back details of what will be required, while the other will comfort them, softening the facts, focusing on the relationships, and offering hope. It would be natural for Mary to want to make sure this complementary expression of consolation is included when Jesus describes the coming trials of her children.

By entrusting Mary to the beloved disciple and to all disciples, Jesus has given his church a compassionate mother. As Mary met with the disciples in the upper room and lived as part of this new community, perhaps she spoke words similar to these departing words of Jesus to console the church. And if Mary indeed influenced the composition of John, then a gospel dominated by the themes of sorrow and separation followed by the joy of reunion and rebirth is exactly what one would expect from the mother of the Messiah. A mother knows well that the birth pangs are followed by the joys of birth. John and Mary reflected together on the words of Jesus and helped the disciples incorporate them into their hopes and prayers: "So you have pain now; but I will see you again, and your hearts will rejoice, and no one will take your joy from you" (verse 22).

The spread of Christianity depended heavily on its attractiveness to women. Women in the ancient world resisted various forms of sexual servitude and violence and the abhorrent exposure of infants that was so common throughout the Roman empire. Christianity served as a great "feminist" force, raising the dignity and status of women. Only Christianity professes that a human woman gave birth and became a genuine mother to the transcendent God.

Another of the many ways that we see the influence of Mary in John's gospel is the significant role played by women from first to last: Mary at Cana (chapter 2), the woman of Samaria (chapter 4), the woman taken in adultery (chapter 8), the mother of the man born blind (chapter 9), Martha and Mary at Bethany (chapter 11), Mary anointing Jesus at Bethany (chapter 12), the women at the foot of the cross (chapter 19), and Mary Magdalene heralding the resurrection of the Lord (chapter 20). As Christians met in house churches, in Jerusalem, Ephesus, and wherever the church was established, we can be sure that Mary was present when the church gathered. As the community remembered and reflected on the women who influenced the life of Jesus, Mary's input would not have been insignificant in those encounters. Surely, she must have insisted that her new spiritual sisters should be included in John's presentation of the good news of her Son.

Reflection and discussion

- How might the insights of Mary have influenced the Christian assembly in the house churches of Ephesus?

- How does the image of childbirth help me to understand the meaning of the suffering I experience in life?

- In what ways has the gospel message elevated the status and dignity of wives, mothers, and single women?

Prayer

Coming Lord Jesus, your followers weep and mourn while the world rejoices. Teach me the message of your cross, the pain that will turn into joy. May the consolation of your mother be the voice that moves my heart with joy.

He said to his mother, "Woman, here is your son."
Then he said to the disciple, "Here is your mother."
JOHN 19:26–27

The Mother of All Disciples

JOHN 19:25–30 ²⁵*Meanwhile, standing near the cross of Jesus were his mother, and his mother's sister, Mary the wife of Clopas, and Mary Magdalene.* ²⁶*When Jesus saw his mother and the disciple whom he loved standing beside her, he said to his mother, "Woman, here is your son."* ²⁷*Then he said to the disciple, "Here is your mother." And from that hour the disciple took her into his own home.*

²⁸*After this, when Jesus knew that all was now finished, he said (in order to fulfill the scripture), "I am thirsty."* ²⁹*A jar full of sour wine was standing there. So they put a sponge full of the wine on a branch of hyssop and held it to his mouth.* ³⁰*When Jesus had received the wine, he said, "It is finished." Then he bowed his head and gave up his spirit.*

The mother of Jesus, a few of the women from Galilee, and "the disciple whom he loved" remain near the cross of Jesus. This beloved disciple is traditionally identified as John, the apostle and writer of the gospel. Everyone else has fled the scene out of fear, shame, or confusion. Only these few followed Jesus faithfully to the end.

Although no one has Mary's maternal attachments with her Son, and Jesus has unique emotional attachments with her as his mother, they have both grown to love the disciples dearly. So, at the cross, immediately before his saving death, Jesus unites his mother and his beloved disciple. "Woman, here is your son," he told his mother. "Here is your mother," he told his disciple.

According to the perspective of John's gospel, Jesus gives birth to his church at his death on the cross. Although the mother of Jesus and the beloved disciple are historical figures, at the cross they represent the new family of faith. The beloved disciple is developed as a representational disciple throughout the gospel. He is the model disciple and the ideal witness to Jesus. In giving his mother to the beloved disciple and his beloved disciple to his mother, Jesus is giving her as mother of all disciples and giving all his disciples into the care of his mother. In this mutual exchange, Jesus is clearly doing more than just providing someone to look after his grieving mother when he is gone. Jesus entrusts her as the spiritual mother of his church.

Throughout John's passion account, Jesus is presented as the royal Messiah, a true king, though mocked with a purple robe and crown of thorns. "Here is your king!" Pilate announces, yet Jesus responds that his kingdom is "not from this world." Scourged, stripped, and nailed to the cross, Jesus seems more like a total failure than a king. But Mary is being challenged to see what John's gospel proclaims—that the crucifixion of Jesus is also his enthronement. And thus, the mother of the Messiah, though not a queen in this world, is truly the queen mother in the kingdom of her Son, exercising maternal care over his church.

The two appearances of Mary in John's gospel, forming bookends at Cana and at the cross, interpret one another. Although the "hour" had not yet come at the wedding feast, the "hour" has arrived at the cross. This is the time of the birth pangs, foretold by Jesus to his disciples: "When a woman is in labor, she has pain, because her hour has come" (16:21). For his disciples, the hour is a moment of deep suffering that will be followed by great joy, like the experience of a mother who gives birth to a child. As Mary stands with her dying Son, she exemplifies, more than anyone else, this sorrow that will lead to rejoicing. The pains and joys of childbirth are embodied in Mary's experience at the cross. So, as Jesus surrenders his life, he offers his mother to his disciples for their mutual consolation. At this same "hour," Mary becomes the mother of the church: "From that hour the disciple took her into his own home" (verse 27).

At Cana, Mary trustingly told her Son, "they have no wine," and Jesus provided choice wine in abundance for the thirsty guests. At the cross, Jesus says, "I thirst," and he is given the sour wine of Calvary in the presence of his mother. Immediately afterward, Jesus utters his last words: "It is finished." As he died, the text tells us, Jesus "gave up his spirit." The Greek words literally mean "he handed over his breath/spirit," indicating that there is more here than simply a euphemism for death. Jesus pours out his Spirit upon his infant church gathered beneath the cross, offering them a kind of sober intoxication, which is life lived in the Holy Spirit. As he let go of his own life, he breathed life into this new family of faith. The last breath of Jesus was also the first breath of the newborn church.

The lifting up of Jesus on the cross is the turning point of salvation history, the hour of the Messiah's triumph over Satan, "the ruler of this world," and his demonic powers. The moment harkens back to the messianic prophecy of Genesis in which God declares to Satan: "I will put enmity between you and the woman, and between your offspring and hers; he will strike your head, and you will strike his heel" (Gen 3:15). In each of the appearances of Mary in the gospel, Jesus addresses her as "Woman" (John 2:4; 19:26), the title of the Messiah's mother whose offspring will mortally wound the serpent who brings sin and death to the world. Mary is the archetypal woman of Genesis, the new "mother of all who live." She is the mother of all who are spiritually alive in Christ through grace.

Reflection and discussion

- How can Mary's example at the cross of Jesus offer me hope in times of trial?

- If John's crucifixion scene demonstrates that Jesus is a true king, though "not from this world," what does this indicate about the royalty of Mary his mother?

- How does John's gospel show Mary to be the mother of every disciple of Jesus?

- How are the sufferings of the Messiah and the sorrows of his mother part of the birth pangs that give life to the church?

- In what ways am I a part of the new family of faith that Jesus formed at his cross?

Prayer

Crucified Lord, in your dying you have poured out your Spirit upon your people and brought your church to life. Give me grace as I seek to be your beloved disciple and help me to experience the love of Mary, the mother of your church.

Then the dragon stood before the woman who was about to bear a child, so that he might devour her child as soon as it was born.
REVELATION 12:4

The Royal Woman in the Heavenly Temple

REVELATION 11:19—12:11 ¹⁹*Then God's temple in heaven was opened, and the ark of his covenant was seen within his temple; and there were flashes of lightning, rumblings, peals of thunder, an earthquake, and heavy hail.*

12 ¹*A great portent appeared in heaven: a woman clothed with the sun, with the moon under her feet, and on her head a crown of twelve stars. ²She was pregnant and was crying out in birth pangs, in the agony of giving birth. ³Then another portent appeared in heaven: a great red dragon, with seven heads and ten horns, and seven diadems on his heads. ⁴His tail swept down a third of the stars of heaven and threw them to the earth. Then the dragon stood before the woman who was about to bear a child, so that he might devour her child as soon as it was born. ⁵And she gave birth to a son, a male child, who is to rule all the nations with a rod of iron. But her child was snatched away and taken to God and to his throne; ⁶and the woman fled into the wilderness, where she has a place prepared by God, so that there she can be nourished for one thousand two hundred sixty days.*

⁷*And war broke out in heaven; Michael and his angels fought against the dragon. The dragon and his angels fought back, ⁸but they were defeated, and there was no longer any place for them in heaven. ⁹The great dragon was thrown down, that ancient serpent, who is called the Devil and Satan, the deceiver of the whole world— he was thrown down to the earth, and his angels were thrown down with him.*

126

¹⁰*Then I heard a loud voice in heaven, proclaiming,*
"Now have come the salvation and the power
    and the kingdom of our God
    and the authority of his Messiah,
for the accuser of our comrades has been thrown down,
    who accuses them day and night before our God.
¹¹*But they have conquered him by the blood of the Lamb*
    and by the word of their testimony,
for they did not cling to life even in the face of death.

A s John's vision reveals the heavenly temple, the ark of the covenant is seen amid the sights and sounds of a divine revelation (11:19). As the chosen vessel of the divine presence in the old covenant, the golden ark contained the tablets of the Torah, the manna, and Aaron's staff. As the Israelites journeyed through the wilderness, a cloud, signifying the presence of God, would descend upon or "overshadow" the tent where the ark was kept. Yet, at the time of Jesus and his church, the ark of the covenant had been missing from the temple for six centuries, and God's people awaited the disclosure of the ark of the new covenant.

As we've seen, the New Testament reveals that Mary is the new ark, the divinely created bearer of the Messiah, bearing within her virginal womb the incarnate Word, the Bread of Life, and the eternal priest of the new covenant. The account of Mary's annunciation describes the cloud of God's glory that will overshadow Mary, the divine sign awaited by the Jewish people for the revelation of the ark (2 Macc 2:8; Luke 1:35).

As John's vision continues (remember, there are no chapter divisions or verse numbers in the original text), a pregnant woman appears in the heavenly temple giving birth to the Messiah (Rev 12:1–2). The true ark of the covenant is no longer on earth but in heaven. For the author of Revelation, the new ark of the covenant and the woman clothed with the sun are dual images of the same person, the Blessed Virgin Mary.

"A woman clothed with the sun, with the moon under her feet, and on her head a crown of twelve stars" is clearly a regal image. The crown is a symbol of royal authority and victory. Isaiah describes Lady Zion as no longer needing the light of the sun or the moon because she will be illumined by God's glory (Isa 60:19–20). The bride in the Song of Songs is described as "fair as the moon, bright as the sun" (Song 6:10). In Joseph's dream, the sun, moon, and stars bow before him, representing the royal authority he would be given over his father, mother, and brothers when he would arise as the most powerful person in Egypt's royal court. The twelve stars point to the woman's relationship with the twelve tribes of Israel or with Christ's church, founded on the twelve apostles.

Although the visionary portrays the woman in ways that recall both Israel and the church, presenting her as a representation of God's people, he more specifically depicts her as the mother of the Messiah. Her Son is the king exercising his universal dominion. The messianic imagery of Psalm 2 is used to describe how her child will "rule all the nations with a rod of iron" (verse 5). Her Son is taken up to heaven to God's throne, and he ushers in the kingdom of God as the enemy is defeated (verse 10).

The royal mother, portrayed alongside her royal son, evokes the Old Testament tradition of the Great Lady (the *Gebirah*). She is the mother of the king in the line of David, giving birth to her son, and remaining closely associated with her son throughout his reign. This queen mother is the mother of Christ and the mother of his church. The regal woman is also the royal mother of the Emmanuel prophecy of Isaiah, the queen mother who will give birth to a king in the line of David (Isa 7:14). Just as the young mother of the king is described as a divine "sign" given to the house of David, a "sign" as "high as heaven" (Isa 7:11), so the vision of the royal women in Revelation is described with the same language: "A great portent [*semeion*, in Greek] appeared in heaven" (verse 1).

The royal mother's childbearing pains do not depict the agony of physical birth (verse 2). They are, rather, the agony Mary shared with her Son at the cross, the pain of labor that comes at the hour of new birth, the suffering that will be turned to joy (John 16:21). This is the pain foretold by the prophet Simeon as the child Messiah was brought to the temple, saying to Mary that her Son would be "a sign that will be opposed" and that she herself would be pierced with a sword (Luke 2:34–35). She continues to experience the pain of being the mother of the Messiah and of his persecuted church.

In this final image of the mother of the Messiah in Scripture, we see how the mother of the Lord fulfills the Old Testament. As the new "mother of all who live" (Gen 3:20), she is truly the mother of all those living the new life of grace in her Son. The first Eve succumbed to the temptation of wanting to be like God and sinned, but Mary is full of grace and free of all sin, submitting to the will of God: "Let it be with me according to your word" (Luke 1:38). Following the sin, God said to the serpent, Satan, "I will put enmity between you and the woman, and between your offspring and hers" (Gen 3:15). In Revelation, we find Satan represented by a dragon, "that ancient serpent, who is called the Devil and Satan, the deceiver of the whole world" (verse 9). Although the enmity between Mary and Satan continues as the dragon is thrown down to the earth, the victory of her offspring over the demonic powers is assured. The defeat of the forces of sin and death is won by "the blood of the Lamb," the atoning death of Christ and the courageous witness of his followers (verse 11).

This rich image is a beautiful expression of the role of the Blessed Virgin Mary in God's plan of salvation. She is the new mother of all who live, the ark of the new covenant, the royal mother of the Messiah. Since the Annunciation, Mary's task was to give birth to Christ, to nourish and protect him as he grew into a man. Likewise, since the crucifixion, Mary's task is to give spiritual birth to Christians, to nurture, guard, and guide them into the full stature of Christ. The royal mother of the Messiah is the queen of heaven and earth.

Reflection and discussion

- What most convinces me that the woman clothed with the sun is an image of Mary?

- How does the woman clothed with the sun depict the royal mother of the Messiah?

- What is the role of the Messiah's mother in the church's ongoing battle against the powers of the dragon?

- Which image of Mary in Scripture offers me the most hope?

Prayer

God of heaven and earth, you have revealed the salvation you have given to your people in heaven as we struggle against Satan on earth. Through the powerful intercession of the mother of Christ, strengthen your church as we await the fulfillment of all your promises.

SUGGESTIONS FOR FACILITATORS, GROUP SESSION 6

1. Welcome group members and make any final announcements or requests.

2. You may want to pray this prayer as a group:
   Incarnate Lord, you have come to share our humanity so that we may share in your divine life. From the cradle to the cross, your loving mother has accompanied your saving life. Give us the grace to reflect on the holy mysteries of your saving life through the heart of Mary so that we may reflect her love for you. Help us embrace her as our own mother so that we may experience the consolation that gave joy to the heart of your beloved disciple. May your blessed mother reign in heaven as the mother of all your church.

3. Ask one or both of the following questions:
   - How has this study of Mary enriched your life?
   - In what way has this study challenged you the most?

4. Discuss lessons 25 through 30. Choose one or more of the questions for reflection and discussion from each lesson to discuss as a group.

5. Ask the group if they would like to study another topic in the *Threshold Bible Study* series. Discuss the topic and dates and make a decision among those interested. Ask the group members to suggest people they would like to invite to participate in the next study series.

6. Ask the group to discuss the insights that stand out most from this study over the past six weeks.

7. Conclude by praying aloud the following prayer or another of your own choosing:
   Holy Spirit of the living God, you inspired the writers of the Scriptures and you have guided our study during these weeks. Continue to deepen our love for the word of God in the holy Scriptures and draw us more deeply into the hearts of Jesus and Mary. We thank you for the confident hope you have placed within us and the gifts that build up the church. Through this study, lead us to worship and witness more fully and fervently, and bless us now and always with the fire of your love.

Ordering Additional Studies

AVAILABLE TITLES IN THIS SERIES INCLUDE...

Advent Light

Angels of God

Divine Mercy

Eucharist

The Feasts of Judaism

Forgiveness

God's Spousal Love

The Holy Spirit and
Spiritual Gifts

Jerusalem, the Holy City

The Mass

Missionary Discipleship

Music, Hymns, and
Canticles

Mysteries of the Rosary

The Names of Jesus

Parables of Jesus

Peacemaking and
Nonviolence

People of the Passion

Pilgrimage in the Footsteps
of Jesus

Questions Jesus Asks

The Resurrection and
the Life

The Sacred Heart of Jesus

Stewardship of the Earth

The Tragic and
Triumphant Cross

Wholehearted Commitment
PART 1: Deuteronomy 1–15
PART 2: Deuteronomy 16–34

Jesus, the Messianic King
PART 1: Matthew 1–16
PART 2: Matthew 17–28

Jesus, the Suffering Servant
PART 1: Mark 1–8
PART 2: Mark 9–16

Jesus, the Compassionate
Savior
PART 1: Luke 1–11
PART 2: Luke 12–24

Jesus, the Word Made Flesh
PART 1: John 1–10
PART 2: John 11–21

Church of the Holy Spirit
PART 1: Acts of the Apostles 1–14
PART 2: Acts of the Apostles 15–28

Salvation Offered for
All People: Romans

Proclaiming Christ
Crucified: 1 Corinthians

Unity in Christ's Church:
Colossians, Philemon,
Ephesians

New Covenant Worship:
Hebrews

Faith, Hope, and Love:
The Seven Catholic Epistles

The Lamb and the Beasts:
The Book of Revelation

TO CHECK AVAILABILITY OR FOR A DESCRIPTION
OF EACH STUDY, VISIT OUR WEBSITE AT
www.ThresholdBibleStudy.com
OR CALL US AT **1-800-321-0411**

**TWENTY-THIRD
PUBLICATIONS**